BEING RIGHT HERE

T0198495

ཞབ་ཕྱག་མཁན་འགྲོའི་གསང་མཆོད་ལས༔

རྟོགས་པ་ཆེན་པོ་ཉམས་སུ་བླང་བའི་ཁྲིད

དོན་གསལ་མེ་ལོང་

བཞུགས་སོ༔

BEING RIGHT HERE

A DZOGCHEN TREASURE TEXT OF

NUDEN DORJE

ENTITLED

THE MIRROR OF CLEAR MEANING

WITH COMMENTARY BY

JAMES LOW

Snow Lion
Boston & London

The lung of the root text given by H.H. Chhimed Rigdzin Rinpoche, the lineage holder of this text and reincarnation of the treasure finder Nuden Dorje, is available through **edition khordong**, Berlin. edition@khordong.net, www.khordong.net

An **edition khordong** production,
the publication house of the nonprofit Khordong e.V. in Germany.

This teaching was given by Ven. Dr. James Low from the 23rd till the 27th of July at the Pfauenhof Retreat with and on request of Chhimed Rigdzin Rinpoche in 1998, Germany.

Transcription by Olaf Brockmann and Ruth Kürmann
Edited by Andreas Ruft
Corrected, completed and authorised by James Low

Based on the terma (*Don gSal Me Long*) of Nuden Dorje Drophan Lingpa Drolo Tsal (*Nus lDan rDo rJe 'Gro Phan gLing Pa*), edited by Khordong Terchen Tulku and Chhimed Rigdzin Rinpoche

The root text (*Don gSal Me Long*) was first translated from Tibetan into English by Chhimed Rigdzin Rinpoche and Gudrun Knausenberger. A revised translation was done by James Low.

The line drawings are by Leho Rubis, Estonia.

Snow Lion
An imprint of Shambhala Publications, Inc.
Horticultural Hall
300 Massachusetts Avenue
Boston, Massachusetts 02115
www.shambhala.com

Printed in the United States of America

⊛ This edition is printed on acid-free paper that meets the American National Standards Institute Z39.48 Standard.
♻ Shambhala Publications makes every effort to print on recycled paper. For more information please visit www.shambhala.com.
Distributed in the United States by Penguin Random House LLC and in Canada by Random House of Canada Ltd

Designed and typeset by Andreas Ruft, Berlin

ISBN 978-1-55939-208-2

Cataloging-in-Publication data is available from the Library of Congress.

CONTENTS

Contents

Don Sal Melong

PREFACE

This brief commentary is offered as a gesture of welcome to the view and practice of *dzogchen*.

The root text is written by Nuden Dorje (*Nus-lDen rDo-rJe 'Gro-Phan gLing-Pa Gro-Lod rTsal*) in the mid nineteenth century. It forms part of his collection of treasure teachings. These are teachings that he first heard in his former incarnation as Khyeuchung Lotsawa (*Khye'u-Chung Lo-Tsa-Ba*), one of the twenty-five close disciples of Padmasambhava, the great tantric master who created the integrated style of Tibetan Buddhism. Nuden Dorje spent most of his life in Kham in East Tibet where he spent many years in retreat. A master of *tantra* and *dzogchen* he was known for his quick mind and penetrating understanding. The text was translated with the guidance of his forth incarnation Chhimed Rigdzin (1922-2002).

Chhimed Rigdzin Rinpoche and Gudrun Knausenberger worked on a first draft of the translation of the root text. Rinpoche asked me to look at it and make improvements. I did a re-translation of the text during a brief but very happy stay with them in Offenbach near Frankfurt. I was able to ask Rinpoche many questions in order to gain a precise understanding of the lineage reading.

The text provides a very clear authentic account of the view and essential meditation of *dzogchen*, the practice of non-dual experience. The presentation is in the *Men Ngag* style, a personal instruction distilling the authors own realisation, revealing the lived experience of the *terton* Nuden Dorje Drophan Lingpa in a manner both beautiful and profoundly meaningful.

7

Preface

The text is very fresh, radiant with the dew drops of its short lineage. Like a flower or a beautiful piece of art it will reveal itself to those who open to it with a quiet mind and a heart softened through tender attention. It consists of short verses which, with pithy clarity, show how the various aspects of *dzogchen* fit together. The text provides both an authentic account of the practice and instruction in how to apply it.

Dzogchen, often considered the highest level of Tibetan Buddhism is an ancient system of realising ones own authentic nature. The tradition of transmission is unbroken and this text provides a traditional consideration of the key points of the system. It speaks to the heart of the human condition, highlighting the need to integrate all the aspects of ones being, overcoming fear, anxiety and denial.

The commentary was made at Rinpoche's request during his retreat and teaching at Pfauenhof to students of the lineage. My comments express the mood of the time. The commentary has been only lightly edited to keep some of the flavour of the event.

It provides both an expansion of the traditional concepts embodied in the text and an examination of how they can function in modern everyday life. The commentary explains key practices and how to manage difficulties that arise in meditation. There are of course many more ways of approaching this text which is so rich and deep. I think it would help readers to also study chapters 8, 10, 11 of 'Simply Being' which address many of the problems which can arise during this kind of practice.

Giving this commentary was the last time I taught in Rinpoche's presence and rereading it brings back the facilating warmth and spaciousness of his empowering and liberating display. The teacher is the site of integration; through the practice of the text the nature of life is revealed through integration with the living presence of the teacher. The teacher is of course not an entity but a relational field.

8

Don Sal Melong

Many people have contributed to the production of this small book; all our efforts mingle with the efforts of others. In particular Andreas Ruft has been the guiding force of the project, diligent, calm and enthusiastic.

May all our busy work
Bring you rest and ease.

James Low, London, April 2003

Note of the editor

All Tibetan and Sanskrit terms except proper names are placed in italics. Tibetan terms are transcribed in brackets on their first appearance, using the Wylie system as modified by Chhimed Rigdzin Rinpoche. The root consonant of each syllable has been capitalised in order to avoid any ambiguity.

The editor would like to thank all people who have contributed to this work, especially Ruth Kürmann and Olaf Brockmann for transcribing the teaching, Leho Rubis for providing the line drawings, Wolfgang Zimmermann for his steadfast constancy and Snow Lion Publications for making this teaching available to a larger audience. Last, but not least, our thanks go to our beloved teacher Chhimed Rigdzin Rinpoche who entrusted us all with this deep and meaningful teaching of his heart. None of this work would be possible without his generosity.

Padmasambhava

Introductory Invocation of Padmasambhava

སྐྱབས་གནས་བསླུ་མེད་དཀོན་མཆོག་རིན་པོ་ཆེ།

ཐུགས་རྗེ་མངའ་བའི་ཨུ་རྒྱན་པདྨ་ལ།

བདག་གིས་རྗེ་ལྟར་གསོལ་བ་བཏབ་པ་བཞིན།

 གྱུར་དུ་འགྲུབ་པར་བྱིན་གྱིས་བརླབས་དུ་གསོལ།

To the precious jewel who is my unfailing refuge,
Urgyen Padma who has compassion;
I pray for the blessing that whatever I request
May be quickly accomplished.

Seven Line Prayer

ཧཱུྃ༔ ཨོ་རྒྱན་ཡུལ་གྱི་ནུབ་བྱང་མཚམས༔

པདྨ་གེ་སར་སྡོང་པོ་ལ༔

ཡ་མཚན་མཆོག་གི་དངོས་གྲུབ་བརྙེས༔

པདྨ་འབྱུང་གནས་ཞེས་སུ་གྲགས༔

འཁོར་དུ་མཁའ་འགྲོ་མང་པོས་བསྐོར༔

ཁྱེད་ཀྱི་རྗེས་སུ་བདག་བསྒྲུབ་ཀྱིས༔

བྱིན་གྱིས་བརླབ་ཕྱིར་གཤེགས་སུ་གསོལ ༔

གུ་རུ་པདྨ་སིདྡྷི་ཧཱུྃ༔

Hung. In the north-west corner of the land Urgyen,

Hung. In the north-west corner of the land Urgyen,
Upon the stem and stamen of a Lotus,
Are you who have the most marvellous and supreme attainments
Padmasambhava of great renown,
With a retinue of many Dakinis around you.
Following and relying on you I do your practice, therefore,
In order to grant your blessings, please come here.
GURU PADMA SIDDHI HUNG

Refuge and Bodhicitta

ༀ། །སངས་རྒྱས་ཆོས་དང་ཚོགས་ཀྱི་མཆོག་རྣམས་ལ།

།བྱང་ཆུབ་བར་དུ་བདག་ནི་སྐྱབས་སུ་མཆི།

།བདག་གིས་སྦྱིན་སོགས་བགྱིས་པའི་བསོད་ནམས་ཀྱིས།

།འགྲོ་ལ་ཕན་ཕྱིར་སངས་རྒྱས་འགྲུབ་པར་ཤོག།

To the Buddha, the Dharma & the Sangha
I go for Refuge until Enlightenment
By the merit I have created through generosity and other virtues
May I gain Buddhahood in order to help all sentient beings.

INTRODUCTION

𝕿his afternoon we were taking refuge with Rinpoche and the final refuge we said was: "I take refuge in my own mind." Now we can say that all together and then try to work out what it means.

"I take refuge in my own mind."
"I take refuge in my own mind."
"I take refuge in my own mind."

In the next four days we will have time to look into this text "The Mirror of Clear Meaning" (*Don gSal Me Long*) in order to understand more what it means to take refuge in one's mind.

If it is raining you can take refuge in your umbrella against the rain. You have a simple desire to keep dry. You have a simple enemy – the rain. And you have a simple friend – the umbrella. This is the basic principle for buddhist refuge. We have suffering as the principal enemy, we have the teachings of the Buddha as the main protection and we have ourselves that we are trying to protect. And we protect ourselves because we want to be happy and we imagine there are things that make us unhappy. So the things that make us unhappy affect us. If we can find a way to protect ourselves from the things that affect us we will be happy. But when we look into this, it is of course always complicated. Who is the one that we are trying to protect and who is really causing trouble for us?

In all the levels of Buddhist teaching it says very clearly that it is we ourselves who cause trouble for ourselves. And what is the bit of ourselves that causes trouble for us? It is our mind. So our mind is causing us all our problems and at the same time the highest level of refuge is to take refuge in the mind which is causing you all your problems. Mind is the cause and beginning and the site of *samsara* and it is also the site and the experience of *nirvana*. But the way that this term 'mind' is used in Buddhism is different from our ordinary sense. What is meant here by 'mind' is not our ordinary sense of me: 'I, the thinker'. It is more the felt presence of our own existence and this presence of our own existence is not something which can be identified as being an object.

So now we will go through the text. In the first verse it starts to explore the ground of the view, the basis of the view of *dzogchen (rDzogs Pa Chen Po)* and with this we will move into the discussion of the preliminary practice.

）

VERSE 1

– THE VIEW OF DZOGCHEN –

རིག་སྟོང་གདོད་ནས་དག་པ་རྱུང་འཇུག་ལམ༔

གྱེན་གྲུབ་སློས་པའི་མཐའ་བྲལ་ཡེ་ཤེས་རྒྱས༔

རང་རིག་ཡེ་སངས་རྒྱས་པ་ཀུན་ཏུ་བཟང༔

རང་ཞལ་མཇལ་བའི་མན་ངག་འདི་ཕོ་ནༀ

> *"Using this secret instruction one can see one's own face, one's awareness which is the primordially enlightened Samantabhadra. The unitary path of primordial purity of awareness and emptiness spreads as the spontaneous wisdom free of all relative conditions."*

𝕿his first verse is such a wonderful verse because what it is saying is that from the very beginning this natural presence or awareness has been completely merged with emptiness. And the nature of this fusion of emptiness and awareness is completely pure. Each of these terms has many meanings and I start to unpack them a little just now. When it says awareness and emptiness, *rigtong (Rig sTong)*, this *rigpa (Rig Pa)* or awareness is our simple being when we just sitting here – somebody is here. Before we know who we are being here, this somebody who is just here gives us the beginning of the flavour of this term awareness or *rigpa*. We could just take a moment to observe ourselves. Here we are sitting, however we are sitting, whatever way our body is. We don't have to sit in a special way to look at it. Somebody is here. Without thinking about who you are being here just try to have the sense what is this presence that you are. Sit with that for a few minutes.

Okay. Something is there. You don't have to know what it is but something is there. And there is also a sense of change. There is some connection with energy. In the way that it is changing you can already get a sense. It is maybe difficult to say exactly what it is. This quality, this nebulous quality, this difficulty of grasping this natural presence as being any particular thing is a quality of its emptiness. So this presence is a noetic presence, a presence of awareness through which all the different aspects that we construct – ourselves and our world – arise. It is the medium of the experience that we have. And depending on our relationship with this medium the experience reveals itself as *samsara* or *nirvana*.

The text says that awareness is pure from the very beginning. *Dodne dagpa (gDod Nas Dag Pa)* means this has always been pure. Time is very important. We experience our lives through the medium of time. We think about what we will do in the morning, we think about what we will do tomorrow. When we meet somebody new, we introduce ourselves in terms of our past and if we like them, and we want to do something with them, we immediately start to make some fantasies or plans for the future.

Attachment is temporal. It is a quality of time. To be attached to things involves trying to stay with particular people or objects as we move through time. And identity is also related very clearly to time. We are our history. But the text is talking about the nature of the of mind, the real nature of mind as something which has been there for infinity without any beginning at all. That is before we were born, before our parents were born, before our countries came into existence, before the big bang, before the universe came into existence. That has always been there. Now clearly we are already aware of the Buddha's teaching on impermanence: that everything that is created moves towards destruction and change. But if this real nature that we have is infinite, it means it was before there was any beginning. And in not having a beginning it will not have an end. Without a beginning or an end it cannot be an entity. And this is not just an abstract concept. This means we are not entities. We are not things. So that means we are not who we think we are.

Going back to the refuge. When we take refuge in this nature of our mind, we are taking refuge in the true nature of our self, which we don't know. And we do that in order to get rid of the ordinary identity of who we know we are because we don't like that. That is really something to think about. If you are successful and you get enlightened you will not be who you are now. *You* will not get enlightened. The one who gets enlightened will not be *You*, as you know yourself to be.

This nature of the mind, the text then goes on to say, is arising spontaneously free of any limiting points. These limiting points are the ways in which we start intuitively to have a sense that something exists as an entity and this state is suffused with wisdom. And the quality of wisdom is that it doesn't get tied in knots. We all have a sense with Rinpoche that it is very difficult "to pull the wool over his eyes", or trick him. He has good sense of what is going on. That is a quality of wisdom.

Then the text goes on to say that our own awareness is only natural presence, is the primordial buddha *Kuntu Zangpo* (*Kun Tu bZang Po*), *Samantabhadra*. When it says *Kuntu Zangpo* it is meaning both *Samantabhadra* and *Samantabhadri*, this couple. This couple has been there for a very long time and they form a little world of their own. They are like springtime lovers in Paris. This is very important because when we start to recognise the nature of our mind, we become distracted. Although we can have moments of being truly present and quite open, quickly we become distracted or attracted to something else. We betray emptiness and go off seeking some busy lover who will leave us anyway. So ordinary love, ego love is fickle. But the love of this primordial awareness is very, very reliable. And this couple, being together, this is a real symbol of the possibility of attaining a state of complete integration with all that arises without leaving it for distraction.

The text then goes on to say that this is a text which is designed to show you, to introduce you, to your own face, to your own nature. We are all sitting in this room with a face but we have never seen our own face. If you look around you can see other people's faces very easily. It is quite ridiculous that it is very easy for me to see, for example Robert's face, but I can't see my own. I mean that seems completely ridiculous, it is *my* face and I can't see it and I spend all my life looking at other people's faces and not at my own face.

There are many terms in Tibetan which are around the sense of my face: *rang ngo (Rang Ngo), rang she (Rang bZhin), rang sha (Rang Zhal).* These terms are all on this point that this thing which is always there, which is us, is completely hidden from us although it is always there and it is us. And if you want to see your own face you have to look in a mirror. You see yourself as a reflection with the left-right inversion. And in seeing yourself in a mirror you see yourself as something other than yourself. Seeing ourselves in a mirror supports us in the sense of being an entity.

In child-psychology there are many developmental theories which talk of how the ego sense of self develops through being mirrored by other people's eyes or by actually looking in a physical mirror. And even in the path of *tantra*, when we get an initiation and we get the teaching that now you are *Tara*, now you are Padmasambhava or *Vajrasattva*, you see yourself in another form. And that form in a sense reflects your own good qualities or possibility of transformation. But it is still one step removed – you become other than you are. But this text is saying that it will show us our own face, so that we will see our own face directly! This might indicate that in order to see our face directly we have to look in a different way.

Then the text moves on to preliminary practices which are designed to stop us looking at our face in the usual ways and then it starts to show how to look in a new way.

20

Don Sal Melong

So first we will discuss some of the general views in Buddhist practice and then go through the preliminaries, because I want to look at the preliminaries through the view of *dzogchen*. We can look at the preliminaries through the view they have of themselves but we also can look at it through the *dzogchen* view.

Hinayana, Mahayana

Generally speaking the Buddha's teaching begins with what is called the *hinayana* path where the focus of attention is separating out from *samsara*. In this approach to the world you spend a lot of time reflecting on how horrible life experience is. We do that in order to subvert or disrupt the pattern of our usual investment of meaning in the ordinary things of our world. For example you might reflect that the body is full of pus and blood, disgusting substances, worms and shit and by looking at other people as being a bag of such substances your desire for them would be diminished.

If we want to give up *samsara* and want to get out of it, it is always much easier to think about the faults of others. In this part of renunciation all the things, all the objects that stimulate the senses and which pull us into desire or pull us into anger and rejection, anything which creates an intensification of our connection with the world needs to be stopped. Because the goal is to become cool and free of the heat of the passions, so that we just trickle over the edge and vanish.

However in the *nyingma* view that we try to practice, we take the key elements of this view of renunciation and integrate them. Rather than really believing *samsara* to be a difficult place, we use this idea as a tactical pressure to try to dislodge the pattern of our own attachment. That is to say we use the attitude as a method to help us be less involved in our ordinary obsessions so that we have more space to recognise something of the true nature of our existence. And then in the *mahayana* path we are developing wisdom and compassion together and we do this again in order to create more space. If we commit ourselves to helping other people we will not be able to do this if we continue to be self-obsessed.

The View of Dzogchen

In the *hinayana* path we are saying the world is bad and we want to get out of it so that the conflict is between ourselves and the world. But in the *mahayana* path we try to internalise the conflict so that our aspiration to be good and to help other beings is in conflict with our *karmic* traditional tendency to take care of ourselves. If we put other people first after a while we will start to hate them. It is one thing to think about saving all sentient beings, which is a very beautiful abstract concept. But if you are sitting in the *puja* and you are trying to meditate and the person next to you is bumping your knee or singing out of tune or banging the bell in the wrong rhythm you might feel some irritation. And the real issue in the *mahayana* path is struggle, that one commits oneself through millions of lifetimes to engage in an ongoing process of helping others. That is to say direct engagement with the manifestation of limitation, and the purification of it through wisdom.

In the *hinayana* path the basic motive or model is that of the renunciant, the person who leaves their family, who leaves their home and goes off casting the world behind them. In the *mahayana* path the main motive is that of the servant. One gives away one's freedom in order to become a servant for others. But at the same time this is a servitude which brings pleasure, because the key for entering into it is the understanding of emptiness. So we have to get some understanding of emptiness otherwise a real commitment to be at the service of other beings will simply be torture for ourselves and will in fact then cook up our own five poisons even more intensely. This is very important. If you are walking along the river and you see someone falling into the river if you jump in to save them that is very nice. But if you can't swim it is not very helpful. From this *mahayana* buddhist point of view unless you have some understanding of emptiness it is all just empty words. The *dharma* is just so many nice fairy tales where we pretend that we are all going to be good people and help others but actually we spend our time taking care of ourselves, and our fantasies.

Tantra

In the path of *tantra* there are many different subdivisions. But as a general style of practice the task that we are trying to do, the key task, is to transform the five poisons into the five wisdoms. And in order to bring about this experiential transformation, we use identification with the deity. We use the blessing power of the deity, the richness and complexity of meditation with all the aesthetic supports for that: *tanka*, music, dancing, colourful clothes and so forth.

Now if we want to transform these five poisons, we have to have the five poisons. Probably we could agree we all have the five poisons. But a lot of the time we don't know we have them. So they are difficult to transform. Even in the path of *tantra*, although a lot of the practice is through visualisation and using the richness of the practice to support one-pointed attention, which starts to liberate us from the usual destructive preoccupations that we have, we still need to be able to see things as they are in order to transform them into something else. Because the task is a revisioning.

For example in the *Big Rigdzin (The Vidyadhara Guru Sadhana, terma* of Nuden Dorje) practice towards the end there is a section that comes from the *Leudunma (gSol 'Debs Le'u bDun Ma)* where it says: 'Regarding all these objects that you see, good things and bad things, our practice is to see these as the form of the *gurus* body, form of Padmasambhavas body...' And we hold to that. But clearly this is also a path of effort because we will have a habitual tendency to see things as we are accustomed to seeing them. When we look around the room we say: "Oh, I know you. I met you before. You are Robert." You don't immediately think: "Oh, this is *Vajrasattva*."

So what we have is the flow of our *karma*. In Tibetan it is called *rang gyud (Rang rGyud)*. *Rang* means ourself and *Gyud* just means like a stream or a flow, the same word that we use for *tantra*. This stream of our own ordinary perceptions is what ties us into the world. In *tantric* practice as this is manifesting we are putting another identification onto it. So it is as if *karma* or our past is bringing meanings to us and we are transforming these meanings into the *mandala* on the moment of their arising. And

9

23

The View of Dzogchen

then whatever appears as resistant to this transformation that we try to make, we understand this is a demon. And that is why in Tibetan Buddhism there is a lot about demons.

Some of you have just been on a *Vajrakila* retreat and *Vajrakila* is very concerned with putting the nail in. So wherever there is a demon or an entity *kila* goes into that and dissolves it. I don't know if it happens in Europe but certainly in Canada, in the old days when they were cutting down the forest they would run tree trunks into the river. And there would be men who would stand on these tree trunks with a stick and they would keep pushing at the logs to keep them turning so that they would flow down the river. This is essentially the function of *Vajrakila* because when we become *Vajrakila* we keep the river free, we keep the stream of life going. This is the practice of *tantra*. Everything keeps manifesting in this light, free form, and wherever the logs could come together, wherever the river of experience could get blocked and we start to build up something, give it a 'bang' and it moves on again. And in the *Big Rigdzin* there are many moments where you have a similar kind of thing where we use different kinds of positioning, threatening, beseeching, bribing to try to get our demons to move on.

Dzogchen

So we can maybe see that throughout these different levels, the *hinayana*, the *mahayana* and the *tantra* that the key concern is with dynamic movement and the key enemies are points of stasis around which constructed senses of self and world are build up.

Now the practice of *dzogchen* is rather different. Although it is often woven in with these three, the particular position it takes up is different. Because it starts with this view, as we described from the first verse, that from the very beginning everything has been perfect. This is the meaning of the name of this wonderful couple [*Samantabhadra, Samantabhadri*], 'Always good'. And because it is always good therefore it is never bad. Very simple. So if you think it is bad that is because you have not realised that it is always good and when you recognise that it is always good

Don Sal Melong

it stops everything bad. The proof of enlightenment in this path is that you end up having a real good time. That is very important because at the heart of the *dzogchen* practice is the notion that there is no need to make any effort because things are already perfect.

Our habitual tendency is to imagine that our duty is to improve things, to improve ourselves, to improve the world and as we looked in these other systems, the *hinayana*, *mahayana* and *tantra*, there is still this tendency that if you don't do something it is not going to improve. But *dzogchen* begins with this statement that from the very beginning everything has been perfect so there is nothing to improve. If you are involved in any creative arts, I think you will find that when you do a painting or you write a poem or make a pot and you want to improve it then you make it a mess. We need to trust our intuitive relation where we see: "Oh, that's fine!" and stop there. *Dzogchen* is about developing an intuitive aesthetic relationship with the world. And here the world includes ourselves in which we try to be our relaxation, to let everything go free. But of course we don't need to let things go free because things are already free but we imagine that they are not free so we are going to set them free. Learning to give up unneccesary effort is difficult because so much of our identity is based on activity, on doing things.

The key issue is how can we get into the direct experience of this flow of reality in which there is nothing to do. And not only to enter into it but also to enter into it with the confidence that by relaxing control we will in fact be increasing our ethical relationship with the world and our manifestation will of itself be good without our trying to be good. But of course good here doesn't mean good in relation to bad. It is talking of an infinite quality of simple perfection and it will take us perhaps some time just to get the flavour of it.

But I suggest we take a short pause now and get some fresh air and maybe in that if you are just walking in the air just try to very gently have this felt sense: "What does it mean to be me?" It is not a question to ask round and back on yourself but just from the inside out. "What does it feel like to be me? What is this 'me-ness' of me?"

Function of Ritual

One of the things we do when we come into the room we make prostrations. Even if there is a break in the *puja*, people go out and when they return they make prostrations because when we begin a retreat this space becomes constituted as the mandala of the *guru* and in this sense it becomes a sacred space. And by gaining initiation and by gaining devotion and appreciation one is able to attune oneself to the sacred quality of the space that is established, to the energy that is created here and you use that in the practice of transformation. This is perfect in the practice of *tantra*.

In the practice of *dzogchen* there is a slightly difference. If we say that from the beginning everything has been perfect and that is the view we seek to hold, if you then make one space sacred then by definition an other space is profane, and so you are causing a split and a judgement in that which is from the very beginning always being perfect everywhere.

There is a lot to think about the function of ritual when we come to hold a view which is definitely non-dual and grounded in a notion of natural perfection. But of course since we anyway make the meditation of prostrations in the state of emptiness we ourselves are empty, the *guru* we prostrate to is empty and the act of making prostrations is empty, it does not really matter too much. If you don't have the view and the real understanding of that emptiness then you have potentially some problems. It is just important to be aware of this because the mood and the attitude in *tantra* are very much about respect. In *tantric* vows there is a great deal about respect for the *guru*, respect for women as a principal of the *dakini*, for many, many things in order to built up this rich sense that this world is already an enlightened *mandala*. That is to say: In *tantra* we are imbuing, we are filling activities with added significance, added meaning. We are enriching them from the source of the symbolic.

But in *dzogchen* we are trying to experience the nakedness. The simplicity of the natural perfection of things is the reason that they are without need for alteration in any way. So the mood is more relaxed and that may appear to some people as being not so respectful and even more disrespectful. But at the heart of *dzogchen* practice is awareness and if we are aware in what we do, it doesn't matter too much what we are doing. Because from the view of *dzogchen* the value of anything that occurs doesn't lie in the quality of its content but in its ground and because the ground of everything is pure, everything is pure and has equal value.

Meditation of 'A'

Now we will do a simple meditation using the sound 'A'. The Tibetan alphabet like the Sanskrit alphabet has 'A' as a vowel present in all the consonants. So 'A' is seen as being the mother of all sounds with all other sounds being modifications of 'A'. 'A' is seen as primary and basic and as the letter which represents emptiness. When babies are born they often make the sound of 'A' and then later they develop this as "Mama" and "Papa". And when the Mama and the Papa were making the baby they also make the sound: "Aah, aah..." So 'A' is really quite important. 'A' is what brings us into the world. And when we die we go out of the world with the 'A'.

In *dzogchen* there is a great deal of attention to energy and to the felt sense that everything in the universe has a particular vibration and sound. By using this sound 'A', which is seen as having a very root vibration, a vibration of the very basis of consciousness, it helps to shake the other vibrations back into line. Because from this view everything which manifests is a variation on 'A'. If we can see the link back into 'A', we can see how everything arises out of this sound 'A' and so can be brought back into this ground nature by allowing the sound of 'A' to spread out. So we can use the sound of 'A' to radiate out and to make connection with everything. For everything is a manifestation of the potentiality of the ground nature of the inseparability of awareness and emptiness.

In this practice we can visualise in our heart the white letter 'A' (using either the Tibetan form ཨ or the capital A) and in the space in front of us another white letter 'A' and then we recite "Aaaaa" together and in that we keep our awareness on these two letters 'A'. Then after some time you just let these 'A's relax until one is simply unified with whatever is there. Ordinarily we exist in the little world of our sense of being a separate self and this sense of separation has a particular vibration that we return to again and again. But now we use 'A' to return to our deeper home. I think we often can experience this around Rinpoche. Sometimes when we hear his voice or even just feel his presence it can put a little shaking in us so that things settle down. So we try this practice with the goal of being very relaxed and present. There is nothing really to achieve here. It is more like a return ticket. You have already gone somewhere, so we use the 'A' as the second bit of the ticket just to get back to where we started from.

Don Sal Melong

Sitting comfortably not straining the body with this very relaxed sense of the 'A's' we recite together. You are not looking at the wall in front of you, you are just letting your attention hover in the space in the middle and imagine this 'A' there. If it is difficult to imagine an 'A' then just let your attention hover in the space in the middle. When we relax into this space it is not our space. Nobody has appointed you to be a policeman for this space. So if thoughts come you don't like, you have no right to 'arrest' them. If some feelings come and 'park themselves illegally on your pavement', just let them stay there. Whatever comes is not your problem.

(Recitation of the three 'A's', then silent meditation for a while)

With this kind of practice it is not an issue of having a good meditation or a bad meditation. It is just something that we do. We often have a great desire to have a good meditation, to be very fresh and very clear, and then we are upset if we have bad meditation which is sleepy and unclear and full of thoughts. To find ourselves worrying about our meditation is a sign that we don't know how to meditate. Patrul Rinpoche has a very nice text on the faults of meditators in a chapter in the collection 'Simply Being'.

I suggest we do this three 'A's' again and whenever you are ready to, come out of the state of 'A' and get on with doing something else. But whatever you are going with, if you take the 'A', the flavour of the 'A' with you, the practice will not end.

It is always interesting to see where your mind is when you are waiting for things to begin. So check out what you are doing at the moment.

Who Am I? – General Principle of Dzogchen

The problem that we try to resolve throughout the *dharma* and particularly in *dzogchen* is the problem of location. What is the nature of the site of being? Generally speaking we have the sense that: 'I am living here. I am inside my body. My body is here in this room.' And what is the status of this site? What is it constructed from? If it does not have a solid construction then the notions of self that we rest on it and all the actions that arise out of it will be unreliable.

There are many exercises which have to do with this but the first thing is to investigate the nature of ourselves. In *dzogchen* we are always trying to observe ourselves. Now observing oneself may seem easy. Linguistically it sounds quite easy. It is like: "Observe yourself, observe your feet." And so if we want to observe our feet it is quite easy. We look down and there they are. But if you want to observe yourself, you first have to find your *self* in order to observe it. So in order to find ourselves we have to look for it and if we are going to look for it what are we looking for?

If we accept that we have never seen our own face then what we are looking for is simply a construct of representations and so we may end up looking for our assumptions and then fulfil them. We are used to observe things. And if we observe ourselves in the manner of observing things we will, no doubt, present ourselves to our self as a thing because that is what we have been doing from the very beginning of *samsara*. That is what *samsara* is.

So what we really have to do is to develop a new form of observing the self, one which is more like hanging out with your self. Just being there while you 'self' yourself, observing this process of 'selfing' yourself. Because if *You* are not 'selfing' yourself, who is? In *dzogchen* this is called: "Staying with the one who is doing whatever is going on." If thoughts are arising stay with the one who is thinking the thoughts that are arising. If feelings arise stay with the one who is feeling the feelings. If no thoughts and feelings arise stay with the one who is completely dull and stupid. Because the one who is doing this activity is existing somewhere. Where does it exist? If you watch carefully you will be able to see self coming into existence. But if you don't observe carefully then this point of manifestation of the one who is doing will always present itself as if it is an eternal site of self: "I am me!" And my grasping at this one closes the door to liberation.

The key problem is that from the beginning the mind has been open, very relaxed, unborn, uncreated and yet the experience of the mind has been: "I am me. I am not you. Leave me alone. Give me what I want!" From the very beginning we have not known who we are. Thinking "I am me" means I have not realised who I am. The "me" is the objectified refined point of self, which appears like the cursor point on a computer, the little arrow, the thought that shows you where you are and like this little point on the computer it is not anywhere, it has no true existence. It is on the screen. The screen is not anywhere. It is like liquid crystal, a dot matrix revealing the illusory realm of cyberspace.

Or in a traditional example: If you look in the sky and you see a bird flying across you see the point of the nose of the bird. But where is that point? The bird is there moving through the sky. It leaves no trace in the sky and you cannot catch the point where it is because it is always moving on. What we call: "Oh, there is a bird flying through the sky!" is a movement. We construct the notion of the bird. What we observe is a movement.

In the same way the nature of the mind is to be very creative. Thoughts, feelings, sensations are ceaselessly arising and we ourselves put these into positions and locations, juxtaposing one to another and through that creating the illusion of the separation of self and other. Although we can say generally speaking that *samsara* began a very long time ago, if you really want to see the point where *samsara* is arising, look in your own mind! And the point where *samsara* arises is the point where there is no one being aware of the one who is doing the thinking, the feeling, the sensation. Who is doing it? Well, I could say who is talking now:

Don Sal Melong

I am talking! And it is very simple. It is me! I know I am talking because I like talking. So I have been talking enough to know what is the sound of my own voice coming out and going back here into the ear. But it would be much better for me not to know who I am! Because by knowing who I am, I become very lazy and assume that who I think I am is who I am. And so I stop observing. And in that way I pass my life as a friend of *samsara*.

So who is doing this? Nobody can tell me because the doing of it is an experience, it is not an entity. If it is just a case of finding out who the guilty person was you could carry out an investigation. But with this kind of investigation the guilty person doesn't exist. So you need a different kind of investigation and this investigation is unlike a police investigation. It is a friendly investigation! Because if you can make friends with yourself, kiss yourself and tickle yourself, you start to relax. And then if you become very good at it you can 'make love' with yourself and you will become all dissolved and then you don't cause yourself anymore trouble. This is the general principle of *dzogchen* and that pleasure, relaxation, letting go, ease, trust, spontaneity, these delightful qualities are the path.

Refuge and the Practice of 'A'

In the *mahayana* tradition when we think about the *bodhisattva* vow it is generally divided in two sections. The first is the intention to act for the benefit of all beings and the second is to actually act for the benefit of all beings. So we start with an idea that: "Yes, I am going to help all beings" and then we actually start to engage in ways which do bring some benefit to others.

There is a similar pattern in relation to refuge in *dzogchen*. We can say: "I take refuge in the buddha." or "I take refuge in the *guru*." The buddha is there and the *guru* is there and now I am making some relation to them in hope that they will provide some protection. The structure of this is about an intention in which the very structure of the intention creates the separation, because you and the thing you are taking refuge in are separate. But what we can also do is to unify ourselves directly with the object of refuge.

The View of Dzogchen

So we can do this short practice of saying the 'A' three times and visualising 'A' in our own heart and in the space in front of us. The 'A' that we visualise in front of us is the essence of all the refuges, of our own teachers, of all the possible refuges there have ever been. It is the unification of all teachers. The first teacher and the most important teacher is our mother who teaches us usually how to walk and how to speak and how to eat. And then we go to school and we have people who teach us all that we have learned as a basis for being able to come into the *dharma*. A basic principle in Buddhism is that all phenomena are connected together through dependent co-origination. And so we want to avoid separating out some of our teachers as being very special and other teachers as having been not that important at all.

We do this practice now, just allowing ourselves very gently to unify with the presence of all the refuges. When we relax the 'A's' and rest in that state, we are actually in the state of ultimate protection, which is the unification of our own state with the ground state of all appearance.

(Saying the three 'A's'...)

Just relax. It's not so bad having a child playing in the middle of meditation because if our own mind is playing it is probably causing a lot more trouble and in *dzogchen* we try to integrate whatever is arising. It is not that we have to hold a stable fixed kind of meditation but to provide some space for experience to arise and pass through. Okay, we return to the text now.

Don Sal Melong

২

VERSE 2

– GENERAL INSTRUCTIONS –

དེས་དོན་སྟོན་པའི་བླ་མ་ལ་བསྟེན་ནས༔

དབང་ལུང་མན་ངག་དངར་ཁྲིད་ལེགས་ཐོབ་ནས༔

དབེན་པའི་གནས་སུ་ཐུན་བཞི་དྲུག་ལ་སོགས༔

རང་གི་ཁམས་བསྟུན་ཐོག་མར་བློ་སྦྱང་གཅེས༔

*"Relying on the Guru who shows you
the definite meaning, having correctly
received the initiations, permissions and
instructions, in an isolated place you
should initially purify your mind during four or six daily sessions according
to the requirements of your own condition."*

This second verse begins by saying that we should rely on
the teacher who instructs us correctly. If you can believe that the

teacher instructs you correctly you don't have to wonder whether you have been taught properly. And if you can then rely on that teaching and that teacher you won't have to think of all the other possibilities, of things you could be doing.

Some of you may know Patrice, member in the French *sangha*. One of his dreams that he talks of many times is to go to a very chic three-star Michelin restaurant and have a very traditional special French dinner. So he will be relying on the chef to provide the definite dinner and if he has a good restaurant and a proper menu well prepared he will then be able to relax because he will have had his dream fulfiled. But if while he is eating his dinner he starts to wonder: "I don't know if this is quite right and also what is this 500 Francs for, it is very expensive," then gradually thoughts will come and his dinner will vanish. It is very important to be able to eat the *dharma* with a good appetite free of distraction and not to leave anything on your plate.

The text goes on: "Having correctly received the initiations, the *lung*, the permission and the instructions, you should go to an isolated practice place and start to do the practice." When we come to a place like this [*i.e. Pfauenhof*], there are many opportunities to study and practice the *dharma* but there are also many opportunities to be distracted. You can be distracted in the meditation, during initiations and just generally in your behaviour around here. If that is the case then what you absorb would be mixed with some kind of lostness, some kind of lack of awareness. Then when you go to sit and do the practice on your own this lack of awareness will be mixed in this practice. And the reality is that Rinpoche is old and sick and one day he will die and then we will cry. But it is one thing to cry because the *guru* is dead. It is another thing to have to cry because you did not learn anything from the *guru*. So it is our own duty to be as aware as possible, because we have no one else to blame.

Having got these instructions we go to an isolated place and do the practice as it says four or six times a day. Usually this means doing the first practice very early in the morning just before cockcrow about four in the morning. It is a very quite time, the world is very still. And then doing sessions of about two hours each doing them through the day. If you do four sessions a day do it about three hours per session.

34

Don Sal Melong

But then it is also saying something very important: "...according to the requirements of your own condition." Because with some kinds of practice, for example doing prostrations or doing a practice where you have to accumulate many numbers of *mantras*, there is a kind of energetic drive, a force of will that you often need to carry you through. But when we practice *dzogchen* we are not forcing ourselves to do something. We are trying to open up a much more subtle relationship with our awareness. So that means we have to be attentive to our own condition, our health, our tiredness, our age, the season, all the factors like that, to see what is the best way for us to do the practice.

ཤ

ༀ

– MEDITATION ABOUT SAMSARA –

འཇིག་རྟེན་འདི་སྣང་མཐའ་མེད་འཁོར་བའི་གནས༔

དུག་མཚོ་ཁོལ་མ་ཐར་བའི་དུས་མེད་པས༔

གཅིག་ནས་གཅིག་ཏུ་འཁོར་བར་རེ་གས་དུག་འཁྱམས༔

ཇི་ལྟར་འབད་ཀྱང་སྡུག་བསྔལ་རང་བཞིན་ལས༔

བདེ་བའི་སྐབས་མེད་ཡང་ནས་ཡང་དུ་འཁོར༔

> *"In this world appearances cease-*
> *lessly flow, in this ocean of poison there*
> *is no time to seek liberation. We wander*
> *again and again in the six realms of*
> *samsara and no matter what we try we*
> *always experience suffering with no*
> *chance of happiness."*

In the third verse here the text starts to discuss what we
should think about once we are in retreat, but of course we can

do this every day. It begins by saying that this world is a place or a site where appearances are ceaselessly flowing. What we call our world is this continuous movement of appearance. Everything is changing around us all the time. If you look at the wall in a room you might generally believe that the wall is not moving otherwise the roof would fall in. But a wall that is not moving is a concept and if you look at the wall you will find that it is moving which is an experience. In *dzogchen* we believe that experience is more important than concept. Most of the points of security in our lives are constructed out of patterns of concepts which we don't examine. When we pay attention to the actual stream of our experience we find that there is very little which is reliable. We often imagine that we are having the experience of a phenomena so that for example if you look at the wall you can have the experience of the wall. But what we call the wall is in fact just experience. There is no wall other than experience. There is a realm of concepts about walls (*samsara*) which we can superimpose on the experience of the wall, which is the wall inseparable from emptiness, arising as the play of awareness and emptiness – the realm of *nirvana*.

This provides us with a clear focus in our practice together: to really come to the point where you believe in experience and stop taking refuge in concept. Because it is through our concepts that we make the false imputation that there is a self-existing essence in the things that we experience.

Then the text goes on that in this ocean of the poisons, the five poisons of stupidity, anger, desire, jealousy and pride, there is no time to seek liberation. The reason that there is no time to seek liberation is because we are fascinated by poison. We are addicted to poison. We cannot tell the difference between poison and healthy things. We devote ourselves to one flavour of poison and then, when it becomes boring or no longer able to satisfy us, we move to another one. So for example you can fall in love with someone and have a lot of desire and think that they are wonderful. But then they do something that offends your pride. So you have more flavours to indulge in. You stop indulging your desire and you start to indulge your pride. But the pride does not stay very long and you get angry. Then you do something which afterwards you think that was stupid. So you are now in stupidity. And the one you loved, having realised how stupid you are, goes off with someone else so that some jealousy comes along for you.

In that way we swim around in this ocean of poison very comfortably. It takes up a great deal of time and while we are having all these, in effect meaningless, experiences the chance to practice *dharma* and recognise the nature of our mind is ticking away as death comes towards us.

Due to this the text says: we keep wandering in the six realms of *samsara* and because of this we keep experiencing suffering. There is no chance of happiness. In Tibetan they often refer to sentient beings as *drowa* ('Gro Ba) and *drowa* means somebody who is in movement or in fact is movement, a mover, something which is in movement. This speaks to the fact that we do not rest anywhere. We are always busy. Busy outside. Busy inside. Moving on and moving on. We have not the power to hold our mind stable for more than a few seconds and are caught up constantly in distractions and things which are very interesting.

Tibetan texts often talk about wandering in *samsara* but this is not like wandering in the Alps with a nice rucksack with some chocolate in it. This is wandering in the sense of not having a definite direction because the path that we take is influenced by so many factors. *Karma* is arising from inside and outside and suddenly situations are arising which throw us off course. So what this is saying is that our very nature is that we are ceaselessly in movement. It is not that we choose to move or choose to stay because even when we stay we hardly stay at all. We are twitching or fidgeting or doing something, for the actual reality of being a sentient being is that we are rarely in a state of simple being. We are sentient doers, reacting, fussing, seeking control and chasing elusive security.*

*) For more explanation of *karma* and *six realms* see chapter 1 in 'Simply Being. Texts in the Dzogchen Tradition' translated and introduced by James Low, Vajra Press, London 1998

Don Sal Melong

– THE OPPORTUNITY OF THIS LIFE –

ལས་ལ་ཟད་པ་མེད་པའི་བག་ཆགས་ལུས༔

ཤིན་ཏུ་རྙེད་པར་དཀའ་བ་དལ་འབྱོར་ལུས༔

རྟེན་བཟང་སྐྱོན་མེད་མི་ལུས་རིན་ཆེན་ཐོབ༔

རྙེད་པར་དཀའ་ཡང་འཇིག་པར་སླ་བ་སྟེ༔

མྱུར་བར་དགེ་བའི་ཚོས་ལ་འབད་པར་གྱིས༔

*"Your body is the remnant of the
karma you have not yet exhausted. It is
the site of the freedoms and blessings
which are so difficult to obtain. Having
gained this precious human existence, a
good base free of faults, so hard to get, so
easy to destroy, you must quickly become
diligent in the practice of virtue."*

𝕿he thing which is probably the most reliable and stable for us in the course of our lives is our own body. Regarding it the text very sweetly says: "Your body is the remnant of the *karma* you have not yet exhausted." In order to get this human body that we have, to be healthy, to be intelligent, to be able to come to a place like this *dharma* centre here and practice, we used up almost all our savings and we have just a little remnant left. And that is being burned up as we move towards our death. So all the good luck, all the good production that we have from the past has given us this rare opportunity but we are not at all that sure what to do with it.

So again it is stressing that this body with this 18 factors of opportunities and freedoms* is very impermanent, doesn't last very long and is the sole basis for really practising the *dharma*. The *dharma* practice that we don't do today, we won't do tomorrow. Because tomorrow we will have tomorrow's *dharma* practice to do and if we did not do our today practice today, why should it be easier to do double tomorrow? So this chance that we have at the moment is seen as something very precious because it is very, very rare.

Now clearly this part of the text is not really the view of *dzogchen*. It is a traditional view of the cycle of rebirth in the six realms but it functions really as a proper preliminary practice because it is designed to wake us up to the absolute importance of being aware of what is going on. It is not a matter of luck that we have ended up with this kind of body. It is the result of actions made in the past and if we do not focus on positive actions now we are likely to have an evil, less viable existence in future.

Whatever security you have in your life, it is very impermanent. When I first met Rinpoche in India he was very strong. He was running around doing many, many things and now for him

Don Sal Melong

---

*) 8 freedoms: not being born in the hells, as an insatiable ghost, animal, long-living god, idiot, in an uncivilised tribe, as one having the wrong view, in a barbarian land;

10 opportunities: to have a perfect human body in a country where the *dharma* has been spread with all five sense organs free of fault, not to have done any of the five boundless sins, to have faith in the pure *dharma*; that a complete perfect buddha has come in the world who taught the *dharma* and the doctrines he taught still remain with the *Arya Sangha* practicing, and is taught by compassionate *gurus* to their devoted disciples. See: 'Simply Being'

to get on this throne in order to teach, people have to push him up. That is the reality. It doesn't matter how many qualities you have. The body has a force of degeneration within it. And the things that we don't do when we are young and strong become more and more difficult to do as we get older and more tired and our health starts to go. There are only two choices: To be aware or to not be aware. And when we are not being aware, we are caught up in the five poisons.

༥

– REPUGNANCE FOR SAMSARA –

Don Sal Melong

ནམ་འཆི་ཆ་མེད་སོས་ཁའི་མེ་ཏོག་དང་ཿ

བར་སྣང་འཇའ་སྤྲིན་ཕོ་ཀའི་བྱ་དང་འདྲ་ཿ

འཆི་བདག་གློག་ཞགས་ལྟ་བུ་མྱུར་བར་འོངས་ཿ

*"The time of your death is uncertain,
for our span is like that of a summer
flower or a rainbow. The god of death
comes as quick as lightning."*

We don't know when we will die is what the text goes on to
describe. Some babies die in the womb. Some babies die naturally in the womb in a miscarriage. Some die as a result of an
abortion. Some die just after they are born. Some have very
grave sicknesses so that they hardly have a life. You can see people die at all ages. We also have no idea how long we will live.
We have the difficult position that we have to take care of ourselves and think of the future and make plans because life
becomes more expensive and as you get old you need to be able

to take care of yourself. But at the same time we don't know whether we will be alive to live off our lovely pension if we get one.

The purpose of these reflections is to develop an awakening that this situation that we are in which can seem so attractive and so seductive and interesting is actually a very, very dangerous place and this is often very difficult to see. A friend says: "Oh, we have not met for a while. Come out let's go and have a drink!" and you think: "Hey, that is nice!" and so you go out and you drink a few beers and you talk of this and that and you think how nice it is to be with this friend. And he is a good friend. So he pays real attention to the stories that you tell him about your life. So you feel understood by him and valued by him. But this dear friend has just poisoned you. Because while he is paying attention to you and is being very interested in your life he was informing you and confirming for you that the petty details of your life are really important. So you get confirmation that your boss at work really is a bastard or that your partner is not treating you properly.

This kind of view which is the basis of our 'being human together' is completely the opposite of practising the *dharma* and this can be very difficult to see. Because we want to have friends and we want our friends to like us and we want to have our good qualities appreciated and we want to have our little pains and upsets comforted. So the factors that go to make for a healthy functioning life are actually factors which go to leave you repeating your existence in *samsara*.

Even in our *sangha* here if somebody says: "I don't know what I'm doing and this has happened..." people tend to listen. They don't say: "Why don't you do some *mantras* instead? It is boring and unhelpful for you to talk this way." That will be considered as very impolite but it would also be very helpful. So it is better being impolite. But we are polite and we allow people to talk nonsense all the time. If you can manage the situation within your *dharma* practice then that is better than an external solution – but beware you don't cheat yourself by imagining you are aware when you are just caught up in what is going on.

Buddhism is not a humanistic viewpoint. It doesn't have human beings as the centre of the universe. It puts awareness at

Repugnance for Samsara

the centre of the universe and those who are not aware are called human beings. So it is very important to think about how we relate to each other. Because if you really develop this sense of repugnance at *samsara* it will give you a functioning protection against the seductions of the mutually self-reaffirming kind of conversation which is endemic in our social life.

༦

Verse 6

– Taking Refuge –

དེ་དུས་བླ་མ་དཀོན་མཆོག་མ་གཏོགས་པའི༔
སྐྱོབ་པ་གཞན་མེད་སྐྱབས་གནས་མ་འཚོལ་བ༔
བླ་མ་སངས་རྒྱས་ཆོས་དང་དགེ་འདུན་ལ༔
དུས་དྲུག་རྣམ་པ་ཀུན་ཏུ་སྐྱབས་འགྲོ་བྱ༔

"At that time you will find nothing to protect you other than the sole protection of the Guru and the Three Jewels. So you might take refuge six times a day or always in your Guru, and the Buddha, Dharma, Sangha."

At the time of your death you will find nothing to protect you other than your *guru* and the Three Jewels. Your mother won't help you. Your lover won't help you. Your children won't help you. Even if they burn some butterlamps they will be thinking about the cost or worrying about the flies that are getting cooked in them.

One of the great functions of the *guru* is to not affirm your value as a human being. The *guru* confirms you as a practitioner of the *dharma* or confirms your moments of awareness but is not particularly interested in the details that you cling to as the basis for your identity. That is very important. In our lives most of the people that we meet are affirming with us our false stories about who we are. So when we take refuge we are taking refuge against our friends. We have to take refuge against our friends even more than against our enemies, because it is easier to see that your enemy is out to cause you trouble. But you need the most protection against your very best friend who is your self, as we talked before.

This practice of renunciation, of turning your back on things which appear attractive is not because we have a basic view in *dzogchen* that the world is a bad place. But it is simply a tactical move to open up a gap for awareness so that the real nature of the world as it is, which is a wonderful place, can be revealed to us. But because *samsara* and *nirvana* are very close together it is very easy to get confused and get the wrong edge.

ཨ

VERSE 7

– THE COMMITMENT OF BODHICITTA –

འགྲོ་དྲུག་སེམས་ཅན་ཕ་མར་མ་གྱུར་མེད༔

སྐྱེན་འཛག་ཀུན་རྟོབ་དོན་དས་སེམས་མཆོག་བསྐྱེད༔

ད་ལྟ་ལུས་རྟེན་བཟང་པོ་འདི་ཐོབ་དུས༔

བླ་མའི་གདམས་དག་མ་ནོར་ཉམས་སུ་ལོངས༔

> *"All sentient beings in samsara have at one time been your parents, therefore develop bodhicitta of aspiration and practice according to relative and absolute truth. Now that you have gained the excellent support of this human existence you must practice the undeceiving instructions of your Guru."*

All sentient beings in *samsara* have been your own mother or father. This means that we have a direct and definite connection with all of these beings. The mosquito who comes and bites you was at one time your own mother or father and when you walk from the garden to come into the puja-room you step on and kill ants on the path, ants which were also your mother or father.

We are connected with the whole world. We are involved whether we like it or not. It is not that we are wonderful people if we take this vow but rather that we are shabby people if we do not. From the traditional point of view we would say it is actually shameful if, having been given the protection of a mother and a father, you turn your back on them. So given that all sentient beings have offered us great service in being our parents it would be just shameful to do nothing for them especially since having met the *dharma* we are able to protect and develop our own existence.

We need to be clear about the relation between the *bodhicitta* of intention, the idea that we will help people and the *bodhicitta* of activity when we are actually doing our best through our practice to benefit all beings. We hope that our practice will benefit other beings but in fact when we try to benefit other beings the main person who benefits is our self. Because if we take seriously this idea that we are connected with all beings and that our duties and responsibilities towards them are not a free choice but are an absolute commitment which is woven into our own history, it is an unavoidable bill which has come back to us. This will constantly awaken us out of the sleep of our own selfish self-concern.

Nowadays the word shame doesn't have a very good reputation. It doesn't have a good feeling to it and in psychotherapy there are many books about problems of shame. But in traditional religious culture shame is very important because it is shame that helps us to awaken to a demand which is larger than our own ego-concern. It is the place where we face the fact that we fall away from the ego-ideal we set ourselves. And in Buddhism that is *bodhicitta*. That shame helps us to break open this sealing of our selfish self-concern. One of the things that we do through the *bodhisattva* vow is to remind ourselves of our connections to all beings so that we include all beings in whatever we do from now on. Thus when you eat you can dedicate your food and imagine that the power of the dedication takes away the pain of all beings. When you have a shower you can do the

Vajrasattva mantra or some other purification practice and visualise that all beings are been purified. When you are in the toilet you can visualise that the five poisons are falling out of the bodies of all beings. If you become a *bodhisattva* you give up having a private life. You become a public person with responsibilities to all sentient beings. And of course we know that the European newspapers make a lot of money out of stories about the secret lives of public people. So if you are going to invite all sentient beings to be with you in everything you do make sure you don't do shameful things.

And again the key focus of this from the view of *dzogchen* is to increase our awareness so that instead of going into a particular activity and being absorbed in it in a dull way, we develop the sense of being open and connected to all beings. With this awareness every activity, every movement and every step we make becomes infinite.

– AWARENESS, KARMA AND VIRTUOUS ACTION –

དགེ་བ་བསྒྲུབ་དང་ཚོས་མིན་སྤྱིག་པའི་ལས༔

བྱང་དོར་མ་ནོར་གཏན་གྱི་འདུན་མ་སྐྱབས༔

མི་དགེ་ལས་བྱས་སྤྱག་བསྒལ་རང་གིས་མྱོང༔

"You must be careful to discriminate without error between the virtuous actions that are to be adopted and the non-virtuous actions which are to be abandoned. You yourself will experience the consequences of your bad actions."

As we looked earlier this world is nothing but a ceaseless flow of appearances which don't stand still. We ourselves are moving, changing all the time with thoughts, feelings, sensations, ideas. The temptation just to get swept along in the flow of these consensual realities is very powerful. If we are going to develop awareness the key thing is first of all to get a clear taste of it, so that having the comparison between how life might be and how life is when we loose awareness, we get a real feeling in ourselves of what a tragedy it will be if we were to continue in this state of habitual unawareness.

The text in the verses 8 and 9 goes on to discuss what happens when we lose awareness. It is talking about how *karma* is generated and created. Generally speaking the idea is that if you perform a good action that will lead to a particular result immediately but it will also lead to a consequence, which occurs later on in time. Nowadays people often talk about instant *karma* but this is not a very traditional idea. Traditionally we think, for example, that if you help someone they may be grateful or you can see that they have been helped. You have a cause which leads to an immediate result but later there is also a consequence whereby something good happens to you. And conversely if you harm someone immediately you can see that they are pained and upset and later some difficulty will come to you.

Although in *dzogchen* one of the goals is to be able to have an experience, a response to the world, that is more spontaneous, this needs to integrate an effortless discrimination of what is good and what is bad. Although we talk of *Kuntu Zangpo* meaning that everything is good, within this sphere of *Kuntu Zangpo*, within this sphere of ceaseless awareness discriminations can be made between what is helpful and what is unhelpful. The key is to separate clarity from the sense that phenomena, including events, are truly existing. Precise discrimination is an aspect of emptiness.

Now, clearly we want all beings to be happy but it may be that we decide that the precondition for happiness is awareness. If that is the case then in order to make people happy we have to help them be aware first of all. It is important to investigate that for yourself because if through your own meditation you come to the conclusion that a state of awareness is really a precondition for happiness then acting to help beings be aware may be more virtuous than offering them the temporary 'happiness' of ego gratification. Though there is clearly an ethical demand inherent in the increased intentionality of this position.

In trying to understand what is a virtuous action and what is not a virtuous action we should consider the traditional definitions of the three unvirtues of body, four of speech and three of mind which you can find described in many books including 'Simply Being'. They work on the general principle of not causing disturbance to self or others. However daily life is not cut and dried.

For example, if you know that it will make someone unhappy if you say something to them about how their behaviour impacts on you and you decide not to say it because you don't want to make them unhappy, that will be to privilege their happiness over your perception of the situation. But you might also feel that if you allow the person to continue within their self-protective activity you are actually preventing them from developing any awareness. They have gone to sleep in habitual behaviour and you have to decide if you will join them in that. If you put awareness at the heart of things it carries with it the responsibility to talk honestly to other people and tell them if their behaviour is an attack on your attempt to stay in awareness.

Something which may appear to be impolite from the ordinary code of social behaviour is actually in terms of the service of awareness a real politeness. We ourselves need to investigate and think about what is virtue, how we are making sense of what is virtuous and what is not virtuous, because human life situations are complicated. There are many factors involved! We are often not very clear ourselves. So it is important to investigate for ourselves.

In general in the analysis of a *karmic* action four stages are described which can help us to think more clearly about what our responsibilities are in any situation. The four parts are the ground, the intention, the activity and the consequence.

The ground is the notion that *I* exist, and with that *I* exist in a world where there are other people who are separate from me and as real as I am. That is to say that the ground of *karma* is the structure of ignorance which is the sense of a separate subject interacting with objects which are real and separate and different.

Many of the practices we do are exactly designed to provide purification on this level. The simple practice of the three 'A's' is very good for this. Also in the *Big Rigdzin* when you take initiation with lights dissolving into the three places, then all together

Don Sal Melong

at the same time followed by the dissolving of the deity into yourself, this process is a way in which subject and object come together and through which you can experience the very essential non-separation of non-duality.

But generally speaking this perception of subject and object is so familiar to us that it appears as normal reality. This is why it is so easy to accumulate *karma*. We start automatically as it were from the presumption that "I am here inside my body looking out at you and we are on the same level as separate and real." In order to get some perspective on this it helps to study traditional analyses of the structures. For example the chapter by Patrul Rinpoche in 'Simply Being' on the two truths is very helpful.

The second of the four stages, the intention, arises in relation to a specific object: I see something and I have an intention towards it. The intention can be one of desire, it can be one of aversion, it can have any of the five poisons running through it.

This takes us into the third stage, that of the activity. In this one engages through action in a relationship with the object.

The forth stage is the completion; the result has been achieved and you consider the result of the action and you agree with it.

With each of these four stages, if we are fully aligned with the stage, that intensifies the impact that it has for our future consequence. Often we do actions and afterwards we think: "Oh, that was not so good." We feel some guilt or some shame and we worry about it. This is very useful because it helps to separate us from the line of the energy of the action and that diminishes the *karmic* impulse. Or we can be starting onto the action and we suddenly decide: "Oh , not such a good idea" and we stop the action without completing it. Or we can be aware at the time when the intention is formulating in our mind. We can think ahead through to the consequences and decide that although it feels attractive, although we can feel the impulse to continue, actually the consequence is not a good one, so we stop ourselves. But clearly we have many intentions forming in our mind all the time and if we are trying to stop things on the level of intention we have to engage in a very intense mental struggle not to get lost.

It is best if we can resolve ourselves on the stage before the intention. That is to say by dissolving the dualistic ground of all *karmic* production into the natural ground of open awareness in which everything arises in the manner of a dream without leading to the separation of subject and object that leads to *karmic* tension. This is very, very important. Because only if you can find a place in your own awareness where you are not caught up in reaction to whatever arises, can you have the calmness and peace which allows the freedom of not engaging in worldly activity. And that is enlightenment.

For example, in the *tantric* style of practice, when we dissolve with the deity it is very important to be as one pointed as possible, to let all our other concerns just collapse into the form of the deity dissolving into us. We move into the ball of light. That ball of light is dissolving because at that point we get to a place which is free of dualism and it is that which is the doorway into an awareness which is uncontaminated. We are turning our back on the world. It is not that we are going to stop doing things in the world. But what we are trying to do is radically relocate the one who is doing the actions that are done. There is one who is aware and there is a point of activity and if the awareness collapses into the point of activity it is always me who is doing it.

54

Don Sal Melong

ℝ

– THE TERRIFYING EXPERIENCE OF DEATH –

འཇིགས་རུང་གཤིན་རྗེས་ལེགས་ཉེས་མཚོན་མ་མཐོང༌༔

འཁོར་བ་གར་སྐྱེ་སྡུག་བསྔལ་ཁོ་ནས་མནརༀ

མཆོག་གསུམ་ལས་གཞན་སྐྱབས་མགོན་དཔུང་གཉེན་མེདༀ

> *"Yama, the terrifying god of death knows all the good and bad things you have done. Wherever you are born you will experience only misery and suffering. Other than the Three Jewels you will find no refuge to protect you or to accompany you."*

𝕋o conclude the final part of the introduction the text emphasises that death is a very frightening experience. As we move into the narrow point of death we are often still connected to all our attachments. Our sense of identity is built into our attachments and as we have to leave our body we can become truly terrified.

Many of you will have experienced the suffering that can arise when a love affair goes wrong. You have invested some hopes and aspects of yourself in an other person and they leave you and you feel as if a part of your life has been taken away. But for most of us after some months or years life goes on and we come back to an ordinary sense of ourselves. But when we go into our death we are loosing the great beloved, which is our sense of self. Our body, our possessions, all the things which we have put ourselves into and which we have used as mirrors to confirm our sense of who we are, all this is shattered and taken from us.

We go into the point of death naked, wrapped only in the protection of our *karmic* clothes. These *karmic* clothes are very dangerous because according to the Tibetan tradition when we go into the *bardo (Bar Do)* the first thing we experience is the open presence of the clear nature of the mind. But because we are covered in our *karma* we get frightened of that. It seems too big, too infinite because we are sure that we are small. 'I am just me. This is too much.'

Then we go into the next stage where the peaceful and then wrathful deities appear to us. But again because of our *karmic* tendency we choose the side of the five poisons. When we start to see the buddha-figures who represent the purification of the five poisons, we experience them as the enemy, either they are too splendid or too terrifying. We cannot recognise that they are the transformation of the very factors, our *karma*, poisons etc., which bind us to *samsara*.

And then in the final stage, where we start fleeing from this experience, we move towards the possibility of a rebirth. There is the tendency to pull our *karmic* clothing around us even tighter, to be more identified with it, and this becomes the point of decision for which of the six realms we are born in.

Hopefully you can see how important an understanding of the nature of ignorance is. Ignorance in Buddhism is a dynamic process that is going on all the time, in which we are ignoring the real nature of the universe, the real nature of our mind. And because we do not see things as they are we continue to develop these illusory beliefs in the habitual forms of our existence and this is what causes the terror of death.

That's why this section talks about *Yama* as the terrifying god of death acting as the judge, who sees our good deeds and our bad deeds. So we need to have more good deeds than bad deeds but also, if possible, and this is the real liberation, to understand that both good deeds and bad deeds are essentially empty.

𝟙𝟘

VERSE 10

– THE LIVING EXPERIENCE OF THE GURU –

དུས་གསུམ་རྒྱལ་ཀུན་འདུས་པའི་རྡོ་རྗེ་ཉིད༔

མཆན་ཉིད་ཀུན་རྫོགས་བཀའ་དྲིན་གསུམ་ལྡན་གྱི༔

རྩ་བའི་བླ་མ་འབྲལ་མེད་སྤྱི་བོར་ཁུར༔

འཕྲད་པར་དཀའ་བ་ནས་མཁའི་པདྨ་འདྲ༔

འཕྲད་གྱུར་གདམས་ངག་ལེན་པ་ཉིན་སྐར་ཚལ༔

ཐུགས་རྒྱུད་གཅིག་ཏུ་འདྲེས་པར་གསོལ་བ་ཐོབ༔

"The embodiment of all the Buddhas
of the past, present and future is your
root guru, the one who has all qualities
and shows you the threefold kindness of
giving you material support, dharma
teachings and enlightenment. So you
should keep him at all times on the
crown of your head with ceaseless
remembrance. To meet such a Guru is

as hard as for flowers to appear in the
sky. To receive his teaching is as rare as
the appearance of stars in the daytime.
Therefore you should pray that you
merge inseparably with his mind."

𝕿his section develops the idea that the real protection that we can have is the presence of the buddha, *dharma* and *sangha* and that their essential form is the *guru*. The *guru* exists in human form giving us the confidence that what we are dis- cussing is not some abstract idea, not a mere hypothesis but what can be a living reality. And if we meet someone with these qual- ities we can have real confidence.

The text talks about the rareness of meeting the *guru* and how you should always act respectfully and be close to him. But maybe the really important line here is the last line: "Therefore you should pray that you merge inseparably with his mind." Believe that the *guru* has understood the nature of his mind, the realisation of the *dharmakaya* nature of mind. If in the meditation we merge with the *guru's* mind and then take that into our every day activity this provides a real protection against absorption in our own historically developed thoughts and feelings. In this sense the *guru* is a tool and it is important to make use of this tool that is available. It is very nice to be respectful to the teacher, to offer things and to smile so that he smiles and you create a nice little world together. But the *guru* has something you do not have. Do you want what he has? Then how can you get what he has?! He wants to give it to you. He tries very hard to give it to you. You want to get it. You try very hard to get it but somehow there is a gap in the middle. So carefully and slowly we need to become full with devotion. We can fill up until we get the direct experience in the meditation of the energy of the *guru's* blessing coming into our heart so that our heart opens and through that we recognise our own nature. But the practice around the *guru* is not a personality cult. You can love your *guru* for all sorts of reasons but the main reason to love a *guru* is as the living embod- iment of the *three kayas (sKu gSum)* and that is what we do in the

Big Rigdzin practice where we do self-initiation with the three lights. This is the unification of the *guru's* mind with our own where he is the living experience when we practice together. He is very open and available and we just try to relax and to tune into that and to feel it coming very strongly.

Don Sal Melong

VERSE 11 & 12

– BUDDHAHOOD IN OUR HAND –

དུས་གསུམ་རྒྱལ་བ་ཀུན་གྱི་གཤེགས་ཤུལ་ལམ༔

ད་ལྟ་སྐལ་ལྡན་གསེབ་ལམ་ཁྱེད་པའི་ཚོས༔

བདེ་གཤེགས་ཀུན་གྱི་ཐུགས་བཅུད་འདི་ཁོ་ན༔

"All the Buddhas of the past, present and future travel the path of these teachings and now you are fortunate to have met this secret path. The heart essence of all the Buddhas is just this and nothing else, the certain secret essence of Ati Dzogpa Chenpo."

རེས་གསང་སྙིང་པོ་ཨ་ཏི་རྫོགས་པ་ཆེ༔

ཕྱིན་ཅི་མ་ལོག་རྟོགས་ན་རྒྱལ་དགོངས་ལོན༔

ཤེན་ཏུ་ལོག་པར་དགའ་བ་ཡིད་བཞིན་ནོར༔

ཤེས་རབ་གསུམ་གྱི་སྒྲུབས་བཙོན་སྟོད་མེད་མཛོད༔

"If you gain an irreversible realisation of this teaching then you gain the understanding of a Buddha. Hard to really understand it is like the wishfulfilling jewel. You must practice the wisdoms of listening, reflecting and meditation diligently and without sloppiness."

These verses are highlighting what it is that the *guru* is presenting. It is not different from the teachings of all the buddhas of the three times*. The *dharma* has just one taste but there are many forms of presentation. With the teaching that we have contained in this text it says: If you gain an unchanging "…irreversible realisation of this…" then you will have gained buddhahood. Buddhahood is not something mysterious that other people have somewhere else, it is actually directly here, you can experience it today. It is just one point. If you recognise that one point, which is the nature of your own mind, it becomes like a wishfulfilling jewel. Everything you will ever need arises from that. If you don't recognise that then you remain in this turning of *samsara*. So it is very, very important that we try our best to recognise this one thing.

First we must listen. This means attend to the teaching as it is. Listen to qualified lineage teachers, study properly translated texts. Attending to the teaching means giving space to it, dropping your own preconceptions and opinions so that a new kind of experience can arise for you, a radical knowledge that can deconstruct your assumptive world. This is the wisdom of listening.

---

*) Three times: Past, present, future.

that state is not our responsibility. This is very important. Because we have this automatic tendency to get in and to be busy, to make something happen. So the key point is to relax. If during the practice you find that your mind is getting busy then just pay attention briefly to your breath. Release some deep breaths from your belly, relaxing the body, releasing all tension and attachment into the out breath, return to presence in awareness and allow thoughts and feeling to come and go.

One of the titles that is given in the Tibetan tradition to a yogi is *jatral (Bya Bral)*, which means free of activity, not being a busy person. The *dharmakaya* itself is very calm and very open and it gives rise to activity for the sake of others. The ground potential offers many, many possibilities. This is the *sambhogakaya*.

Meditation is the experience of *dharmakaya* and *sambhogakaya*. Post-meditation is *nirmanakaya*, the arising of manifest activity in the world for others. It is essential in the practice to trust these three modes even if at first they are not clear. Trust that activity will arise by itself and pass by itself. The self-liberation of experience in all its rich variety, including active and passive, reveals a freedom in activity which is also a freedom from activity.

Then comes reflection, apply what we have learned to our own lived experience. Does it ring true? Use *dharma* concepts to examine your assumptions. Concepts are tools, they have to be put to use. This is an important part of Buddhist practice, applying *dharma* knowledge again and again until it becomes part and parcel of how we make sense of the world. This is an important aspect of taking refuge, learning to use the refuge, putting it to work in a wide range of contexts. This helps us to be clear about the view and to understand the relation between the various views and their associated styles of meditation. Through this one becomes able to differentiate true *dharma* from deluded concepts and comes to be able to trust ones own *dharma* informed judgement. This is the wisdom of reflection.

Meditation is the utilisation of what has been learned and reflected on in the active pursuit of awakening. It is implementation of the specific view one is attending to. Through one-pointed attention to the structures of the practice distraction is diminished, clarity is increased, and openness is revealed. To realise the specific view through the specific meditation is the wisdom of meditation.

Practice of the three 'A's'

Now we do the three 'A's' practice again. Then in your own time gently allow your awareness of yourself in the room to bring you into activity. Take the flavour of that practice with you through eating, talking, being with people. The meditation needs to flow into the world and be inseparable from everything you do.

———————

We will start again by doing the three 'A's' meditation and this time we will rest in the state of openness for a longer period of time. The key is to be relaxed. It is clear from our own experience that we are not in control of our mind. It is then an illusion to keep trying to control the mind. So when we do this practice and integrate through 'A' and relax, our mind is merged in the *dharmakaya* state of the *guru*. Therefore whatever is arising in

Samantabhadra and Samantabhadri

༡༣

– LOOKING FOR THE NATURE OF THE MIND –

ཆོས་རྣམས་ཀུན་གྱི་རྩ་བ་རང་གི་སེམས༔

གང་ཐག་གསར་བུས་སེམས་ཞེས་སྒྲ་ཆེན་པོ༔

དང་པོ་གང་བྱུང་བར་དུ་གང་ན་གནས༔

ཐ་མ་གང་སོང་དབྱིབས་དང་ཁ་དོག་གང༔

རང་སེམས་རྩ་བ་རང་གིས་ཞེ་ཐག་བས༔

ཡང་ཡང་རྩད་བཅད་གནས་ལུགས་གཏན་ལ་ཕབ༔

"Your own mind is the root of all phenomena. When you first start to practice the word 'mind' sounds very big. Where does mind come from, where does it rest and where does it go? What shape is it and what colour does it have? By enquiring into the root of your mind you must again and again come to a definite understanding of its real nature."

"**Y**our own mind is the root of all phenomena." That is a very powerful thing to say! It means clearly that everything that exists in the world has its root in your own mind. So here we are sitting in this room. Each of us is reading this sentence. So each of us comes to the conclusion: "My mind is the root of all phenomena." Very complicated then, because we are each a phenomena for each other. I am the root of all of you for me, but you are the root of me for you and yet somehow we don't bump into each other too much. It is a great mystery and it is a very big question.

Is there one mind with many kinds of plugs going into it or are there many separate totally enlightened minds that are just very good at dancing? It is a very interesting question but also completely nonsense. If you really want to practice *dzogchen* you have to watch out for nonsense questions because you have to keep remembering this distinction between experience and concept. When we go into the realm of concepts many, many things become interesting because each concept is like a mirror which reflects other concepts and through them we come to live in this hall of representations. Clearly in order to understand a text like this and to get into it, you have to think about what is going on. But this requires thinking about it in a way that takes you deeper into the meaning of the text and doesn't elaborate too many thoughts all around it.

As with many *dharma* texts it makes statements: "Your own mind is the root of all phenomena." As a response we need to avoid resting on concepts: "Yes, no, I agree, maybe" and instead to use the statement as a vehicle for investigation of the actual nature of your mind. People who become professors of Buddhist studies find it even more difficult to practice this than ordinary people. I remember when I was first studying with Khipucho I asked him about the role of logic in general Tibetan education. And he said: "Well, if you want to meditate, don't study any logic at all because otherwise it will make your mind so sharp and clear that you will want to attack the faults of others. Spending all your time wanting to cut other people's heads off your own head will get very, very big." This is the opposite of the practice of *Chöd (gCod)*.

When you first hear Buddhist discussion of 'mind', the nature of the mind, mind starts to appear as something very big

Looking for the Nature of the Mind

and not just big but also very important, very real, almost solid. It appears that something very special will happen when I get to the nature of my mind. Because when we don't know what something is but we understand that other people see it as being very important, it is natural that we project all kind of inflating fantasies onto it. The danger is that all these thoughts and concepts, which seem to take you closer to the actual experience, actually take you further away.

Now the text goes on to this basic question: "Where does the mind come from?" 'Mind' here is being used in the ordinary sense of 'you know you have a mind because you know something is going on.' 'Mind' is the shorthand term for this sense of being aware of something. In order to investigate this we can just relax and observe what is going on. Some presence, some attention, some awareness, some something not dead, something alive is there. Ourselves! So what is that? Seems like a very simple question but actually it is quite difficult because we have mind and we have the content of mind and in our ordinary experience mind and the content of mind become fused together. Our sense of the mind is merged in the arisings that are occurring. It seems to have continuity but also a constant change of form.

Shiné – Training in Concentration

We have to start to be able to separate what is occurring from the one who is aware of what is occurring. In order to do that we have to develop a focused concentration or mindfulness so that our attention doesn't flutter and flow into the constant stream of arisings. If you are a beginner in meditation and you find that your mind is wandering a great deal, it is necessary to practice with a simple focus in order to develop the capacity to stay calm (shiné, Zhi gNas). In order to practice clear investigation we have to set up laboratory conditions in which we can hold the frame and limit the number of variables. There are simple ways of helping the mind to focus. We can focus visually on an object outside of ourselves. We can focus on the breath or we can focus on something we imagine.

Generally speaking the external objects are divided in neutral objects, emotionally invested objects and symbolically enriched objects. As an example of the first you could find a small pebble rounded in shape with not a very interesting colour or pattern, just a simple shape to fix your attention on. You place it at a height about level with your heart at about an arms length from you. You allow your attention to rest on it. You could also use the flame of a candle or a butterlamp but the flickering may be unhelpful. In the early days of Buddhist practice they used to make a little disk with clay and put it on a stick, placed at the previously mentioned height and distance.

Or you can use an object which has an emotional impact. In particular people traditionally use a small statue of the Buddha. You could also use a statue of Padmasambhava so that your own faith and devotion toward this image acts as a strengthening factor for the focusing of attention on it.

Or you can use a symbolic object like the letter 'A' or the letter 'Hung'. Usually people use the letter 'A' often white on a dark blue background, and supported by a stick as previously. The distance the object is away from you needs to change depending on the temperature. If it is a very hot day and you are getting sleepy then if the object is too close to you and is causing an intensity of gaze this will increase the likelihood of distraction. So use the distance to the object as a method for helping your practice. With the view of *dzogchen* there are many choices and it is up to you to investigate what works for you.

The answer to the problem of suffering, the real nature of your own mind, will not arrive one day with the postman. You yourself will have to take the teaching and investigate it, so that you have the definite experience. Others give us concepts or some kind of enriched frame, which can optimise the possibility of experience, but we ourselves have to be hungry to gain that experience. In *dzogchen* self-responsibility is privileged very highly. There is very little stress on rules and vows and regulations. The main factor is to understand the principles of how the mind becomes clear and how the mind becomes obscured and then to learn a range of practices, which you can use to keep yourself in clarity.

Where do the Arisings come from?

In looking into the nature of the mind, firstly make sure that you have enough stability and focus in order to be able to do the looking. If you don't have that, do some of the preliminary practices of focusing on the object that have just been described.

When we do *shiné* practice, for example focusing on the breath, keeping the awareness on the upper lip and feeling the breath going in and out or keeping the awareness on the diaphragm as it moves in and out, we have a sense that our mind wanders off. Then we have to catch it and bring it back to the point of focus.

With a simple object outside ourselves or our own breath we collect ourselves together towards the primary focus of attention. Suddenly we become aware that our mind has wandered and so very gently we just catch our attention and bring it back without any blame or faulting to the object of attention. When we have that kind of focus established we can sit relaxed and undistracted and shift the focus to the flow of our experience.

In my experience it is easier for most people to start with the question: "Where do thoughts come from, where do they stay and where do they go to?" We focus on what it is that is occurring in our mind and try to get a sense of where it comes from. How did the stuff get into our mind? After all, we are sitting here quietly inside our little skin bag, and all this stuff is coming in. But when we look for where the thought comes from, we are not trying to find out what was the thought that was there before this thought. Otherwise we trace the lineage of *samsara*, and as many texts say: "*Samsara* is without beginning." So this would take us a very long time. We are not looking at where the thought comes from within the dimension of thought. We are stepping back and seeing the thought coming and having a sense of it when we ourselves are not resting on or identified with thought. In order to do this, the one who is looking has to be very relaxed. With practice the looker is detoxified of its tensions and preoccupations becoming open and spacious, revealing the ungraspable nature of presence.

We apply the same approach to exploring where thoughts rest. 'Thought' in this context includes emotions, feelings and

Don Sal Melong

sensations. 'Thoughts' is being used as a short form for whatever is arising in our experience. We are sitting quietly. Where is this stuff staying? Where does it stay? It is in my mind but what is holding it up? So you have a lot of investigation to do. And then explore where do thoughts, feelings, emotions go to.

It is as if we have been sitting in a very dark room which is very busy for a long time. Many things have been going on but we have never really wondered what they are. We have just taken it for granted: "Oh, this is a thought. Oh yes, they come and go." Just as in the phenomenological method that was developed by Husserl, the key point here is the ability to bracket off assumption so that you can see more clearly what it is actually presenting itself. In Buddhist meditation we need to recognise our many assumptions about the nature and status of our thoughts, feelings and so on and learn to bracket them in order to look freshly at what is actually there.

It might be interesting to sit outside. Relax and take up these questions and explore for yourself what is your way into this and you will start to feel the pressure of assumptions and feel the urge to be distracted and to fall into the flow of thoughts. Then if you think how many hours, months and years of your life you have spent looking at things, being fascinated by things that have now passed away, then how wonderful to spend even five minutes looking into the nature of your own mind.

————————————

Not to be busy

Tibetans say that once upon a time all the yaks that live in Tibet were living in India as water buffalo. It was very, very hot in India so some of them decided if they were to keep walking to the north they would get to a place that would be nice and cool. So they climbed up in the mountains, and as they were climbing their hair started to grow. Because of this the water buffalo in India often turn their head and look out expectantly and they are waiting for their brothers who have wandered off. In a similar way at one time all the buffalo of *samsara* and *nirvana* were living together and one day some of them wandered off

Looking for the Nature of the Mind

and came into *samsara*. They keep looking around to see who else is there and where the other half is, because the basic quality of our ordinary sense of self is that it is very lonely. Something is missing in our lives and we don't quite know what it is, but we keep looking and looking to find this missing part. We can look for it in terms of possessions, we can look for it in terms of the form of our body, trying to change it through dieting or hair style or whatever. You can look in terms of friends. Anything. And this keeps us very, very busy. Sometimes the busyness can be very exhausting, but when we stop then we feel lonely. So we get busy again. *Dharma* is very helpful here if you want distraction because there are many kinds of ways to be busy in the *dharma*. You can focus on having lots of *dharma* possessions. You can focus on learning the text by heart, on the *mantras* and *mudras*, on serving the *tsog*, on doing meditations. There is always something to be busy with.

In Tibet many, many people practiced *dharma* but not so many seem to get enlightened. There are many kinds of *dharma* and if we practice in a way that doesn't focus on the essential point but on secondary and tertiary levels it is easy to get lost. It is really important, given that we have limited time, to focus on what is essential. Many people when they get a plate of food will eat the things they don't like so much first and leave the special thing to the end. But when when we apply this to life we can make a big mistake. The time for deep practice is now. You can learn all about Padmasambhava and what his clothes mean and what his hair style means but if you don't know the nature of your own mind then knowledge about Padmasambhava is just some more concepts.

Looking for the Nature of the Mind

Now we want to focus on what is the nature of the mind. Sit comfortably and we start with the three 'A's' practice. When we relax into the presence of the 'A's', somebody is here, that is to say there is some kind of presence. Where is this presence? Is it resting on anything? Does it have anything outside it? Does it have anything beneath it holding it up? Is it in any way based in a location? We do the practice not for very long for it requires the mind to be sharp.

Generally it is better to do this frequently for 5 or 10 minutes at a time than trying to do it for an hour. When you enter the state of openness, either through 'A' or tantric style dissolving, there is more opportunity to recognise the actual situation because you are quite relaxed and fresh and not so full of yourself. But the longer you go on the greater the risk that you will try, and this effort will of itself create a barrier to the unmediated state.

It is also a very nice practice to do at night when you are falling asleep. It brings a bit of space into the dream.

This verse reminds us that we have to investigate again and again, finding and re-finding the root of the mind until you get a definite understanding. If we had a long time together in retreat we could stop the commentary at this point and continue practising until everybody had some experience and in many ways that would be better, because what the text goes onto next is a statement of the view for which we need some direct experience.

ཉང

Don Sal Melong

– THE NATURE OF MIND –

སེམས་ཞེས་བའི་དང་འདི་པོ་རོས་བཟུང་བླལ༔

དངོས་པོར་གྲུབ་པ་མེད་ཅིང་མཚན་མ་མེད༔

བཙལ་བས་མི་རྙེད་ཡེ་སྟོང་རོས་བཟུང་མེད༔

སྟོང་མེད་བརྗོད་མེད་སྐྱེ་འཆི་འགྲོ་འོང་སོགས༔

རྒྱུ་ཡིས་མ་བསྐྱེད་རྐྱེན་གྱིས་མི་འཇིགས་ཞིང༔

བྲི་གང་འཕེལ་འགྲིབ་འཕོ་འགྱུར་གང་སྟོང་དབེན༔

"What is called 'mind' cannot be identified as this or that. It is not an entity and it has no defining characteristics. If you search for it, it cannot be found for it has been empty from the very beginning, without substantial essence. Empty it is beyond expression, untouched by birth, death, coming and going. It is not created by any cause nor

destroyed by any condition. It remains
untouched in emptiness, free of increase
and decrease, development and decline,
or any kind of change."

This view is expressing Nuden Dorje, it is his *terma (gTer Ma)*, his text, but it also has his presence. It is expressing Nuden Dorje's own experience of the nature of his mind. It is not an objectifying discourse on the nature of the mind. We need to respond to his words in an open way, allowing ourselves to be touched rather than using the concepts to cover over our own mind. The Tibetans say that you can use butter to soften leather but if you keep butter in a leather sack the leather will gradually become dry and brittle. Similarly we can use the *dharma* to soften ourselves, to open up these points of rigidity so that we become very flexible and able to respond to situations. Or we can fill ourselves up with *dharma* so that we become a very rigid pot, being somebody who knows a lot about *dharma*, but actually has no room to move at all. We need to massage the *dharma* into ourselves so that we become soft with it.

Verse 14 begins: "What we call the mind cannot be identified as this or that." When we practice looking where is the mind resting, where does it come from, where does it go, we cannot find any particular thing. There is a lack of some thingness, there is no thingness in this thing which we call the mind. The verse says: "It is not an entity and it has no defining characteristics." A defining characteristic is a characteristic whereby you know that something is what it is and not something else. We can look around here and we can see that each thing in this room has particular characteristics so that we can know what it is. For example most people here have a bell and a *vajra*. And a *vajra* is a *vajra* but each *vajra* in the room is certainly different. If they got all mixed up you would probably be able, if you looked at your *vajra*, to see which one is yours.

But when we look at the mind it does not have these particular qualities. If we try to say that it has a particular colour, we can't find one. If we try to give it a particular shape, sooner or

The Nature of Mind

later it changes from that shape and becomes something else. Sometimes it feels as if our mind is a little point inside our head and it might move around your body or you suddenly feel it is on your left side or behind you on the right side. Whatever it appears to be it is just a moment. A moment of the appearance of something arising in the mind, which is not the mind itself but due to our long established tendencies we very easily confuse the arising as the mind itself.

The text says: "If you search for mind you won't find anything because it has always been empty." That is to say it is not present as something which you can see as an object. It has no objective existence and because it is empty in this way we cannot talk about it, because language is located around objects, around things. In ordinary language we say: "Oh, my mind is tired.", "My mind is sad.", "My mind is bored." or "My mind wants something to do." But when we say that we are saying: "I am having an experience which for me appears to be pervasive and indicates a particular quality of my mind." But the mind itself, is it having this quality? Is the mind itself ever bored or tired or sad?

Clearly some of the experiences which arise in our mind seem to be self-reflexive of the mind, they seem to be referring back to the mind itself. But when we follow that arising, it doesn't seem to lead us to the mind. And this is where we have to be very careful, because this is the point where we can easily tell lies to ourselves about what our experience is. For we are so used to the falsely constructed experience of conflating a concept with an experience. When we do this investigative kind of meditation what we really come to see is just how good we are at cheating ourselves, how many lies we tell ourselves about the nature of our own experience. We fill the space with assumption, with what we know, rather than doing the more difficult work of trying to put the assumption on one side and see what is actually there. But when we really look and we find this emptiness, there is nothing for concepts to cling to and so they pass by, like clouds in the sky self-liberating in their own time and place. Nothing can apply to this and so the mind itself passes beyond "birth and death, coming and going," unchanging. "It remains untouched in emptiness." It is not created by anything and it is not destroyed by anything.

So what we have is this present awareness, because clearly here we are, something is going on, we are all aware of being here. Although the one who is aware cannot be found as a substance it has a tendency to try to identify itself as a substance. Yet this mind itself is not improved by good conditions, it is not made worse by bad conditions, it does not get bigger or smaller, it has never been young, it will never be old. So clearly when you awaken to this, you will be very surprised.

༡༥

– THE GROUND OF EVERYTHING –

མཐའ་བཞི་སྤྲོས་བྲལ་སྟོང་ཉིད་འདུས་མ་བྱས༔

ཡེ་ནས་མ་བཅོས་རིག་པ་ཟང་ཐལ་གནས༔

དེ་རྟོགས་གཞོན་ནུ་བུམ་སྐུ་རྒྱ་རལ་འདི༔

ཆོས་སྐུ་གུན་ཏུ་བཟང་པོའི་རང་ཞལ་མཐོང༔

*"Free of the four limiting notions of
existence, non-existence, both existence
and non-existence, neither existence nor
non-existence, and of all relative positions mind is emptiness, uncompound-
ed. Free of artifice from the very beginning awareness remains unimpeded.
When this is experienced youthful, fresh
awareness is released from its covering
pot and you see your own face, the natural mode of infinite goodness
(Samantabhadra)."*

This verse states that the mind is free of the four basic limiting ideas, ideas which are discussed a lot in *madhyamika* philosophy: of things having an existence, a non-existence, both existence and non-existence, neither existence nor non-existence. These are seen as the four defining propositions of all the possibilities of being. And the nature of the mind is stated to be free of all of these, and all definitions as being this or that.

The next line is very interesting and important. It says: "Free of artifice from the very beginning awareness remains unimpeded." This term artifice, *choma (bCos Ma)*, refers to anything which is constructed. We can examine it in terms of the wheel of life, on the outer circle of which are the twelve *nidanas*, twelve steps. The second of these steps is *samskara*, mental formation, the factors out of which you construct the world and your self. It is represented by a potter's wheel, with which the potter creates diverse shapes, which appear to be separate entities, out of the same source. The first stage in the twelve steps is ignorance. Ignorance gives rise to this busy activity of mental formation, which leads to all troubles of rebirth in *samsara*.

Yet the text says that the mind does not engage in any busyness. Clearly busyness is going on because we are all busy and our activity seems to be quiet real. But this busyness is not a quality of the mind itself. The mind is not busy but busyness arises in an effortless way from it as a ray arises from the sun. As soon as something is constructed it seems to take on not only a shape but a location and if it has a location it is then immediately in juxtaposition or relation to other positions. It is relativised and contextualised. But because the nature of the mind is empty and is not constructed in any way, free of all artificiality, it has no location and so no limit and therefore the text says that it is unimpeded. That is to say it is present everywhere. There are no walls to it because it has no shape or form of itself that would be blocked by an other shape or form.

The nature of the mind is often described as the ground or the basis of everything as we saw earlier in the text. But we have to remember that through our language we are always restricted to these linear and two-dimensional ways of thinking about things. It is not that this nature is the ground existing below things and things rest on the ground. It is not located in relation to anything else. The Tibetan language has developed many technical *dharma* terms with a huge and complicated history and there are many commentaries and detailed references that we can use to understand this text. Yet it is really important to recognise that this text is poetry and we need to read it as poetry because the quality of experience is an aesthetic appreciation, a direct experience. It is not an analytic or intellectual construct. We want to use the poetry to free ourselves, rather than to wrap ourselves in ever more concepts.

When the presence of the awareness is fresh and unmediated, the experience is described as *zho nu bum ku (gZhon Nu Bum sKu)*. This means a youthful pot body. The darkness of a room which has been dark for a million years is removed instantly with one glimmer of light. The freshness has always been there, although we ourselves can feel quite old and tired and our lives are so busy with so many problems. This given nature of the mind which has been there from the beginning of time, being with us at every moment in all the lives we have passed through, has never been touched by any of these experiences that we think have been so heavy, so solidly real. So beneath all the accumulation of knowledge and experience there is nothing but a fresh awareness. Awareness is not touched, shaped, moulded, limited in any way by any of the experiences which we can say it has. But of course it has no experience at all, the one who has experiences is *me*. The nature of the mind 'has' no experience. That of course doesn't mean that no experience occurs, but the one who is 'having' the experience is not there as something as such. This is the illusory play of subject, object and their relationship. So much of our language use is focused on appropriation that it is difficult to express the quality of an open non-appropriative awareness.

It is very important to see this, because all the time we are getting mixed up in things, we are reacting, we are used to be at the mercy of arisings. But the state being described is pure, untouched, virgin and of course Madonna has quite a nice song about that. It is a very good song. If you read the words of that song, it can be a teaching on *dzogchen*: 'In love for the very first time.' Moment by moment the world is fresh to us. Our eyes are open. Our heart is open. Everything is wonderful. Everything is shining. Eternally virgin. Eternally excited and yet quite calm. Not knowing what is going to happen and yet open and trusting. The proof that *dzogchen* is actual is the fact that you can find it in popular culture. How could a teaching on how life is be esoteric? Actuality is everywhere and moment to moment people have experiences of it. Then it gets covered over again. But everywhere in the world people are momentarily opened "hah...huh...gone" and this state is called the *dharmakaya, Samantabhadra*. It is in this that we see our own face. When we see our face we see a face that can't be seen. But when you see it you get quite happy.

Not so solid

Now a little something to do outside when the weather is nice: In Gonpo Wangyal's *chöd* text there is a brief section on *dzogchen* (see Appendix A) and we will focus on a part of that.

Gonpo Wangyal starts by talking of the kind of preliminaries that we have already looked at and then he says: "Outside externally there are stones, rocks, mountains, all of these things and the inner essence of the world, all sentient beings" – this means everything that you can ever see. It means also everything that occurs to you through the senses. It means all of your experiences whether it is of inanimate objects or animate objects and this includes your own physical existence. He says: "All of these things are only names put by your own mind. You must decide that this is exactly the case." This is very, very important for the practice of *dzogchen* because as we started to look last night, in Buddhism there is a great deal of description of the nature of the mind and the qualities of the mind. When this term 'mind' is used in *dzogchen* it means the ground and basis of everything. If we imagine that there are things which are existing outside our mind, the infinite quality of the mind is always going to be blocked by our attachment to these things which we see as being other. When we believe that things exist in reality outside our mind, then we always have a relationship to these objects: "I am thinking about this cup. I am looking at this cup. I am holding this cup." This 'I' exist in relation to this cup. And it means that the precise nature of the cup as something is also making me precise and limited as something. This dualism is covering over the infinite nature of the mind.

So again this is not just a set of concepts. This is a very accurate key into liberating your own experience. It is a practice that we have to do ourselves. Nobody else can give us the result of this. We have to investigate the phenomena that we experience. And we have here a wonderful place to do this. Outside there is water, there is earth, there are trees, there are people wandering around. So go out and really investigate what is there and see that you can understand the way in which you construct this world for yourself. Take an object, a stone and really try to identify what is the basis of the seeming separate existence of this thing. You need to investigate until you get the experience, so that you have the confidence of the experience. You may have studied the theory of this in the past through ideas like the dependent co-origination or through the *Heart Sutra* and so forth. But it is important to have the experience and to use it with everything you encounter. Then you can become free of the belief that there really are separate entities including yourself. Look at the cows, look at the trees and really understand what is a cow! Where is the 'cowness' of the cow?! Who creates the cow that you see?!

It is something to do very often. Hopefully we come to see that words, concepts, naming are floating across the surface of a luminous field. As the power of words and concepts diminishes, the natural radiant vibrancy of the world reveals itself. We also see that words and concepts are also part of this radiance, that they are energy inseparable from the ground emptiness. What we encounter is truly a mystery and we begin to get the sense of why *dharma* texts say again and again that reality is beyond expression, beyond thought.

Gonpo Wangyal goes on to say that having decided that everything is just a name put by your mind, if you then look at the mind itself, it is itself without form or colour and cannot be found anywhere as something to which a qualification or a definition can be put. This is very important because at this point you start to see the beginning of the separation of *samsara* and *nirvana*. When the mind gives rise to language and we take language and concept as real and settle inside them, the glory of the world becomes fixed into boxes within the three times of past, present and future. When we are able at first to relax this flow of conceptualisation, and later to understand its own natural purity, then the world remains, even in the interplay of language, open and beautiful.

So that although language in its conventional form, in its relative truth form seems to be talking about things which already exist, we start to see that it is in fact our reliance on concepts which brings about the birth of these things that seem to be really existing. But it is not that we can say that the language is the enemy, and that we should all take vows of silence. In India there are yogis called *munis* who do that, who decided not to speak. And in psychiatric hospitals you get people who are elective mute. But not speaking is not the answer. We do not find freedom by turning our back on limitations and difficulties. The key point is to relax and integrate all that arises into the state of openness. Integrate the flow of language so that we can recognise that in the moment, when it is moving and seeming to give birth to things, nothing at all is being born. And as we realise this self liberating nature of language, we then are able to speak and to communicate to other people in a way that helps their own use of language to loosen up. There is a lot of work to be done to achieve the non-work of allowing this to arise naturally.

ཕྱེ

VERSE 16
_____

– THE BEGINNING OF SAMSARA –

དེ་ལྟར་མ་རྟོགས་ཤེས་པ་དྲན་མེད་འཐོམས༔

ལྷན་ཅིག་སྐྱེས་པའི་མ་རིག་པ་ཞེས་བྱ༔

སྣང་བ་སྟོང་པ་སོ་སོར་གཉིས་སུ་གོལ༔

གཟུང་འཛིན་སྒྲོགས་ཀྱིས་བཅིང་བས་ཀུན་ཏུ་བཏགས༔

"If that is not realised awareness looses continuity and becomes stupid. This is called 'co-emergent ignorance'. Appearances and emptiness are falsely split and are experienced as separate things. Bound by the fetter of grasping subject and graspable object the ignorance of reificatory identification develops."

In this verse Nuden Dorje is describing the beginning of *samsara*, the nature of the development of ignorance. He says that when we don't maintain our integration in awareness which has been pure from the very beginning, free of any artificiality, then we enter into a realm of stupidity, that is, we ourselves become stupid. This state is called co-emergent ignorance (Lhan Cig sKyes Pa'i Ma Rig Pa). Co-emergent here comes from the Tibetan word Lhan Cig, which means to be born together at the same time.

An example of this would be when you look into a mirror and you see your face; you are seeing a reflection, but you see your face. Two things are there. There is a reflection which is just something on the shimmering surface of the mirror and there is the felt sense that it is your own face. Both are there. But as you shave or put on your make up you are looking at this person who is you. We could recognise that it is just a reflection, but more usually we take the image as real. In this way something arises in the mind which is simply a moment floating through the surface of the continuous stream of energetic arising. But it is seized upon as being something that is existing in itself and so it seems to be pulled out of the state of the mirror into some separate existence. Nothing has actually been removed from the mirror. Everything is as before, just this unborn stream of energetic arising. Unborn in the sense of not being born as a separate entity.

At the same time we have actuality and not recognising actuality. The text says: "Appearances and emptiness are falsely split and are experienced as separate things." And the more we believe that appearances are separate entities any memory or any felt sense of open emptiness is lost and the world becomes more and more complex and fragmented as we experience more and more subtle divisions.

As we are looking into this mirror of experience, which is now full of things, we see the reflection of our self. But the self that we see reflected is also a thing. Because what we see in front of us are things. The more the world is full of things, we, as the experiencer of things, become more sure that we are also a thing.

These external things keep changing and moving which creates a kind of fear for us. We don't want our thing, our basic sense that I exist, to be affected. And the more we encounter change in the external world the more we try to maintain the continuity of this false construction which we are calling our self.

The Beginning of Samsara

We have a sense of a self. This self that we are now creating does not exist as an enduring essence. It has to keep covering itself in clothes in order to give itself a sense of existence. Just as in children's comics when the ghost arrives it puts on a shirt and then suddenly you see a shirt moving across the room. You can only see where the invisible thing is by its clothes and this condemns us to ceaselessly put on new clothes, new concepts, new identities to try to work out where we are. This is the second stage of ignorance in which the mind becomes ever more busy in identifying and constructing 'real' entities to act as a support for its own developing sense that it is a 'real' entity.

ༀ

– 'I' AND 'ME' –

མེད་པ་ལ་འང་ཡོད་པ་བདག་ཏུ་བཟུངༀ

རང་ཉིད་འཁྲུལ་བས་བཅིང་བའི་བདག་ཏུ་འཛིནༀ

ང་བདག་རང་རྒྱུད་ཆགས་སྡང་འཕེལ་བའི་རྒྱུༀ

ཉིན་མོངས་དུག་གསུམ་དུག་ལྔ་འཁོར་བའི་ལསༀ

གཅིག་ལས་དུ་མ་བརྒྱུ་ཁྲི་བཞི་སྟོང་རྒྱསༀ

"Non-existent and existent things are both grasped at as real. Being bound by the confusion of self identification you experience a self doing the grasping. With notions of 'I' and 'me' developing in your stream of consciousness as the cause developing attraction and aversion, there arises the samsaric activity of the afflictions of the five poisons of stupidity, aversion, attraction, pride and jealousy. From one cause

many other causes arise (i.e. all the com-
plexity of samsara)."

"**N**on-existent and existent things are both grasped at as real." The Christian notion of God is a good example of the non-existent. God as an empty signifier can be defined anyway you want – there is nothing visible or tangible to contradict your definition. If you have small children you get used to lying down on the bed with them and beginning: "Once upon a time..." Something comes into your mind and a little story develops. The reason we can do this is because all our lives we do nothing but tell stories to ourselves. We are good at being seduced by narrative and seducing other people with narrative.

The text says: "...bound by the confusion of self identification you experience a self doing the grasping." Thus we start to feel: "Oh, it is me who is doing this. I am the one. Something is going on. Somebody is building this. It must be me." 'I' and 'me' are very interesting terms. 'I' is like a hunter gatherer. It is always out very busily looking at the world trying to bring things home for 'me' who is there cooking the pot. 'I' will ceaselessly find new things to be interested in and to use to construct a sense of a 'me', a stable base to whom experience can be brought.

My self is not a thing, it is a relationship, the relationship I have with myself. I think about myself, I can be proud / sad / fearful / hopeless etc. about myself. 'I' and 'me' are points in a dialogue, a dialogue which strings together a wide range of events, qualities, emotions, judgements, concepts into a seemingly coherent narrative of myself as a confirming and continuous presence. The more sophisticated we are with language the more able we are to deflect the surprises and conflicts that might stop us in our tracks and cause us to question who we are.

You can see how this develops by observing how the children play. For example little Paul is sometimes in the sand pit and you can see that he has a very open smiling face. He goes up to the other children really saying directly "I like you" and then another little child pushes him over and when he falls down he

Don Sal Melong

looks surprised. Something has happened to him. When he was walking over to the other person his face was shining and his body was very open but when he falls down he goes back inside himself. "Something has happened to me." But he is very innocent and very open and he does not have to much memory yet. So his sense of me is not very strong. And he is willingly to try again with an open heart.

When he jumps about he has a full expectation that people will like it and when they laugh he thinks: "Oh, this is lovely." He has very little sense that people might be laughing at him. This innocence is so touching for us because we have lost it. We all have much more history. We have many more wounds. We have very heavy bruises round our heart and so we are much more sensitive about what people think of us. And we are much more sophisticated at playing games of trying to have people like us.

Our painful experiences have brought the five poisons right into our world. Our heavy sense of being a separate person has lead to an anxiety about our safety in the world. This leads us to aversion and attachment, as we long to predict and control our relation with the environment. From this all the other fixed and defensive positions arise. And so the world that we encounter is covered over and suffused with many subtle moods of hopes and fears, doubts, jealousies, pride. So even here on a *dharma* retreat, as we look around the room, we have a complex sense of whose faces we can look at, and who we might have to look away from. This is not at all a neutral place. The force of projections, interpretations and impulsive reactions keeps us busy in trying to stay ahead of the game.

18

ཡིག

Don Sal Melong

– RECOGNISING THE FALSITY –

འཁྲུལ་བའི་རང་མཚང་རང་གིས་རེག་པས་ནི༔
མ་བཅོས་རྒྱལ་མེད་གནས་པ་ཆོས་ཀྱི་སྐུ༔

*"When you understand the falsity of
your confusion remain unartificially,
effortlessly in the natural mode (dharmakaya)."*

What is very important for us to recognise is our own falsity. This is not a judgement that sometimes we are authentic and
sometimes we are false. It means that everything about us in our
ordinary sense of self is false because it is grounded on a misap-
prehension of the nature of reality. Once the original co-emergent ignorance arises, just through the structure of consciousness
that develops with it, everything that we do is false. It is like
somebody in University who is having their final examinations.
They go into the wrong examination room and not reading the
questions very clearly they write very long answers on their own
subject that is unfortunately not the one they are being examined

on. It does not matter how good the answer is they will fail, for they are not addressing the question.

The basic question is always: "Who are you?", "Who am I?" but we do not understand it and so we answer with a ceaseless narrative of self definition. This covers over the freshness of the question, the possibility of looking and seeing, and so all our answers are stale, the reworking of self-protective versions constructed out of unexamined elements. We have many, many, many answers and all of them are false. That's why it is very important when you do the three 'A's' meditation or the other meditations, to put your full energy one-pointedly into the practice, to try to repair the initial basic fault that has torn subject and object apart. It is very important to stop being ashamed of being false. For we have to see how falsity arises, how obscuration develops. We want to look directly at our falsity and learn its tricks so that we will not be caught by them. This helps to open the space in which we can recognise our own nature.

When we do *tantric* rituals such as the *Big Rigdzin* practice we do *Dorje Sempa (rDo rJe Sems dPa', Vajrasattva)* many times and we purify all the sins and faults and mistakes accumulated from the beginning of *samsara*. From the point of view of relative truth we have accumulated a great deal of bad *karma* which, if we don't deal with it, will lead to very painful and difficult circumstances later. Therefore the purification practices of *tantra* are very helpful.

However in *dzogchen* we are trying to get to the essential point where *nirvana* and *samsara* separate. This is like a great weed killer: If you spray it once all the weeds, all the confusion, all the pain and suffering will vanish. You don't need to pluck out each weed by itself. Believing that you are a bad person is very unhelpful for the practice of *dzogchen*. Also believing that you are a good person is not very helpful in the practice of *dzogchen*. You are not a person! Resting in the unborn state we are a pure awareness free of the least defilement. When you give up your ego identity, your *samsara* citizenship, you tear up your identity card and all the problems and sins and police records linked to that identity vanish immediately.

ཉ/ང

VERSE 19

ཨུརཏ

Don Sal Melong

– RELAX, FREE OF HOLDING –

མ་ཡེངས་ཆམ་དུ་ཙོག་གེ་ཞོག༔

དྲན་པས་ཆེད་དུ་བཟུང་བའི་ཚེ༔

གནས་ལུགས་རང་སར་གྲོལ་བ་དཀའ༔

དྲན་རིག་རང་བབ་སོ་མའི་ངང༔

ཆེད་འཛིན་མེད་པའི་རང་དུ་ཞོག༔

"Remain relaxed in the unwavering display of this state. If you try to hold on to it with forced recollection then it will be difficult for the natural condition to be self-liberating in its own place. Keep recollection and awareness in the fresh state of natural occurrence, the state free of strong grasping."

"Remain relaxed in the unwavering display of this state." When we relax through the practice and awaken to ourselves as open presence that rests nowhere and on nothing experiences continue to arise but now as the actual natural display of the state of openness. Ordinarily reality is something that is happening to us. But now we are inseparable from this infinite, unborn, integration within which the sense "oh, I am here having this experience" is part of the manifestation.

Our ego can no longer appropriate the whole show. Having no territory to stand on it comes and goes like all experiences, responsive to arisings rather than trying to maintain a fixed sense of self composed of representations. The sense of finite self is not the centre of the world but is just movement while felt presence is infinite.

"If you try to hold on to it with forced recollection then it will be difficult for the natural condition to be self-liberating in its own place." When you try to make effort or when you do make effort and you try to force a recollection, when you are trying to achieve something then you have a moment of will. You have a subject trying to achieve something by acting on the object domain in order to create for the subject the state that the subject wishes. You already clearly have a strong dualistic polarisation, a condition in which presence is always absent. The key thing is to relax into the openness that is always there. What makes this simple instruction difficult is that it is counter intuitive for the ego.

Relaxation involves a kind of awareness which reverses the normal tendency that we have. Because, as we have seen, this ordinary sense of self that we have lacks inherent self existence, it has to keep constructing itself and that requires a particular kind of effort. The ego's root feeling is that if I do not hold myself together there will be a falling apart into something chaotic and difficult. So there is anxiety, an energetic anxiety which is located in the body, in the whole energetic system of the body and interpersonal turbulence reminds us again and again "If I don't keep it together, I will get in trouble." The belief in reincarnation indicates that for many lifetimes we have been caught up in this anxiety, this nervous contraction which is holding our ordinary grasping sense of self in place.

The text then says : "Keep recollection and awareness in the fresh state of natural occurrence, a state free of strong grasping." You may remember some years ago there was a song by *Frankie goes to Hollywood* and it says: "Relax don't do it if you want to go to it. Relax don't do it if you want to come." This is a song about anal intercourse. As small babies we were shiting in our pants then we learned to tighten our sphincter and we became very proud not to have poo going everywhere. But if you want to have anal sex then you have to be able to relax the sphincter and for many people that is a problem because of the sense of anxiety that comes with going against a strongly established pattern. You have to learn to relax when the instinct is to tighten up and exert control. In some ways *dzogchen* is similar to this because it is going against the impulses of *samsara*. Allowing arisings to happen, tolerating a wide range of experiences rather than editing, privileging and rejecting, is not possible for the ego – only presence, awareness *(Rig Pa)* which is not a construct and is beyond all conditioning is open to what is.

For us it is normal to feel out of control, war, economic change, relationship difficulties, health, there are so many factors which remind us that the stability we seek cannot be achieved by the means we have available. Fear, depression, loneliness, hopelessness – there are many feelings and bodily sensations that we can feel overwhelmed by because they have no place in our familiar sense of who we are. That is why direct introduction *(Ngo-sProd)* is so important in *dzogchen*. Unless we receive transmission and gain a direct experience of our own awareness we will remain caught in a very limited experience of who we are, a state full of grasping and anxiety. It is also very important to observe in yourself where anxiety is located. What are the points for yourself? We all have different patterns in this. What are the points where you become frightened or worried or limited and unable to move into open experience? Observing yourself, looking honestly at the form and manner of your limitations is essential if they are to become allies, aspects of the path to liberation.

ॐ

VERSE 20

– "EAT THE SOUP!" –

བཟླས་བའི་རང་རྒྱུད་མཚང་རིག་ནཿ
གཞི་མེད་རྩ་བྲལ་རང་སངས་རྒྱསཿ

*"If you awaken to the falsity of your
confused existence, you are buddha free
of ground and root."*

"**I**f you awaken to the falsity of your confused existence, you are buddha free of ground and root." Buddhahood is here not something very ornate and elaborate. It is not a construction. It is not sacred or divine. It is simply the revelation of that which has always been, free of causes and supports.

I remember the first time I had an initiation from Rinpoche, a long time ago. I had many powerful experiences during the initiation. Afterwards we went out into the garden in his little house in Bengal and I wanted to ask him about what had happened. But he was calling to his wife: "Amala, bring soup." Then we had the soup and he was talking to me about the soup but I wanted to talk about my experience and he said: "Eat the soup!"

What is important is not to make too much of our own experiences. Of course in the practice of meditation all kind of strange things happen to us. But from the point of view of *dzogchen* everything is to be self liberated for presence has no ground or root. Good things should go free, bad things go free. If we go up to the level of buddha and we have many wonderful things happen to us and we have radiant good health for some time and then we get very sick, we will be unhappy if we have attached to the good state and think: "Why am I now going down?" Enjoyment is different from attachment. Enjoyment is in the moment, attachment seeks continuation of the moment. Relax, be present in the moment, use each moment, each arising as a means of returning to instant presence that rests on nothing.

The more you practice in the view the more everything can become a teaching for you so that any song you hear or food you eat or standing in a queue in the supermarket, everything becomes a revelation of the *dharma*. But as long we know what *dharma* is and we are telling the world "Oh, this is *dharma*, this is not *dharma*" it is very difficult for the natural enlightened *dharma*, which is everywhere, to reveal itself to us all the time, which is the meaning of enlightenment.

Everything changes when we awaken into the lived experience that our awareness is unborn, is not a thing, is not resting anywhere. Then all our assumptions, all the ways of thinking about who we are, we realise to be silly. The beliefs that we have relied on up to this moment, the things that we have thought to be true about ourselves and our world we realise to be false. Instead of helping us, we see that these beliefs have maintained us in confusion. Pure from the very beginning there is no ignorance or consequent affliction. All that arises is self-liberating. Our nature is infinite and beyond conditioning by any impermanent arising. And yet stillness and movements are non-dual and so compassion and wisdom are inseparable as the three modes of the natural condition.

Don Sal Melong

Practice of 'Phat'

There are many different aspects to meditation and each kind of meditation has a particular function, a way of helping us to develop our capacity for non-distraction in the state of presence. For example we need to be able to develop a non-distracted attention through various kinds of fixation, on breath, stones, letters etc. We need to be able to relax and open into a state of fusion and in order to do that we can make use of practice with the deities. We need to be able to integrate whatever arises into the natural state of our own awareness. In the *Longde (kLong sDe)* teachings in *dzogchen* there are many different techniques for this. Bodily yogas, breathing techniques, visualisations, pulse points on the body, different kinds of food to eat, many different teachings on how to manage your energy in relation to the context you find yourself in. The essential practice for this is to find yourself in the state of instant presence and to maintain it whatever happens.

The fourth aspect is subversion in which you try to catch yourself off-balance in order to open up a bit of space. A simple form of this is the practice of using the syllable 'Phat'. There is a lot of detailed description of this practice in the text by Patrul Rinpoche on the Three Essential Points, which is a commentary on Garab Dorje's *(dGa' Rab rDo rJe)* original teaching. There is a translation of that in the collection 'Simply Being'.

Towards the continuous flow of thought, feeling and sensation, our grasping sense of self is marking out: "This is me, this is not me, this is me, this is not me." It is trying to create a clear boundary, a sort of a skin of self which will maintain the illusion of the ongoing separateness of our self.

Modern meteorologists may have a different view but for Tibetans clouds come out of the sky and go back into the sky. And in this sense the sky is like the natural condition itself and the cloud of appearance is coming out and going back into openness. The cloud never leaves the sky, it is an aspect of the sky. You cannot take a cloud out of the sky. The cloud is just there in the sky. But when we look at the cloud we say: "Oh, there is a cloud in the sky" as if somehow the cloud was separate. Or if you look into a mirror and you see the reflection of your own face

"Eat the Soup!"

and then say: "Look , I am in the mirror." What is in the mirror is a reflection, you are not something in the mirror; you are the mirror and its reflection, the stillness and the movement.

When we say 'Phat' we are trying to cut the point where there appears to be a separation from presence and the birth of an entity which is apart from the ground of its arising. By saying 'Phat' we try to shock our mind back into the state of openness, into the mirror-like state, so that the tendency for these concepts to become solid, and the basis for self construction, collapses.

The basic idea is to sit relaxed but with your spine straight holding your skeleton so that free movement can occur inside especially at your diaphragm. You want your belt not too tight. In order to get some basic energy behind it sometimes it is helpful to visualise a small green ball about two and a half fingers below the naval and in equal distance between the front and back or just in front of the spine. And you want to allow this sound 'Phat' to arise from down there. It is not a good idea to shout from your throat otherwise you will get a sore throat and it will make you very tight. And just as sometimes if you have a very good sneeze you get a bit shocked and see balls of light in front of your eyes, 'Phat' can have a similar effect. You don't want to be rough and loud just for the sake of it, practice is not a place to show off, but also you don't want to be timid and frightened. This is a practice of yoga and yogis are people who are shameless in the pursuit of awakening. So we make a commitment to our own naked experience, to clear away all these cobwebs of conceptual thoughts and bring in a fresh new day. Then relax and allow the sound to arise straight through you.

We start with the three 'A's' practice in order to integrate into presence. Then in the state of relaxation when thoughts, feelings and sensations start to come and you experience something like a clouding over or some kind of excitement in which you are loosing your clarity, release the sound 'Phat'. Keep using 'Phat' until there is a bit of space and then relax again into the practice of integration. It is similar to the *chöd* practice for there is really no demon worse for us then these insidious sensations and feelings that arise and which we call ourselves. So we should be quite merciless in this practice of destroying obscuration because confusion will have no mercy on you. It is a shock tactic and you

Don Sal Melong

need to practice it until you experience the 'Phat' arising by itself
with no separation of subject, object, intention and act.

The Function of the Initiation

In the *Big Rigdzin* practice when we practice receiving the
four initiations we use this to develop the possibility of recognising the nature of our mind. Generally when the *guru* is giving an
initiation we try to relax our mind, so that our mind can merge
with the *guru's* mind and the *guru* relaxes his mind out and in
that way the two minds are fused together and that is the direct
connection or transmission.

Although the method is *tantra* there is no real difference
between this and the view of *dzogchen* because having merged
the mind with the *guru* there is more chance to recognise the
nature of your own mind. And when recognised that experience
is not dependant on anything.

In the *nyingma* style there is a double move between *tantra*
and *dzogchen*. The path of *tantra* uses dependency to achieve
transformation. For example in the *Big Rigdzin* we say: "In all my
future lives may I be with you. May I be in your mandala. May
I be close to you. Please hold me close to you." In *dzogchen* the
path is towards liberation in which we loose all dependency and
we recognise that the mind, which is our real nature, is not resting on anything at all but is self-existing from the very beginning.
But there is no real contradiction because if you depend on the
mind of the *guru*, the mind of the *guru* has been unborn from the
very beginning. So your dependency becomes the path of liberation.

Meditation on Machig Labdron

When we do this we visualise her in the sky in front of us.
She is white in colour, dancing. She is smiling. She is very, very
happy. She is looking down on us. She loves us so much. We
pray to her. We love her so much. She wants to save us. We
want to be saved by her. It is very important to pray with an

"Eat the Soup!"

Machig Labdron

open heart, and with hope, excitement and energy. And as we pray to her rays of light are streaming continuously into the body, speech and mind centres of ourselves and all sentient beings. Having received the four initiations all impediments to awakening to our natural condition are removed. So all beings are receiving this beautiful light and purification. The rays of light are also touching the trees, the ponds, the mountains, everything is being transformed by her blessing into a realm of light.

This is very important because the basic view of *dzogchen* is that everything is light, everything is energetic manifestation. We use heart devotion and aesthetic appreciation to open as many centres in ourselves as possible so that we become completely undefended towards this image and can merge fully with it. By the blessing of her rays of light everything is transformed into her nature so that at the end we can imagine all sentient beings merging into our body. Then *Machig Labdron* comes to the top of our head, she dissolves from the feet up and the head down into a ball of rainbow coloured light which then comes down through the top of our head and down into our heart. Then our body, which is now containing all the beings and the whole universe itself and is now made of light, dissolves into this ball of light. So light goes into light. Then the ball of light gets smaller and smaller and smaller until it vanishes into emptiness.

The power of devotion helps us to maintain mindful attention to this ball which is getting smaller and smaller and smaller. Object dissolves into subject and subject dissolves into object and in this non-dual nature they vanish into the basic space and in that state we relax. We just rest in that as long as possible. But of course we carry the deeply embedded energetic tension that I talked of earlier which tends to manifest in this time. So just when you are relaxing you again start to feel this vibration of the desire for subject/object splitting. It is a strong tendency for we have a deep habituation to this nervous anxiety accumulated over many lifetimes. So we should not be surprised if our minds become agitated. Don't worry. As long as we can recognise "Oh, this is the energy of the past, it is coming" something has shifted. Now you have got married to *Machig Labdron* and these thoughts and feelings that come they are like an old lover who telephones you. When you hear that voice you are starting to feel ...ahh.

30

"Eat the Soup!"

But then you look on your third finger and see the little golden band of emptiness and you say: "Thank you for calling, good bye," and so life remains simple. That is the theory.

We do this meditation in order to recognise our own mind. That is why we do it. *Machig Labdron* has no need of anything from us and the only thing that we need to get from *Machig Labdron* is ourselves. So she is not really giving us anything herself. She is giving us ourselves. When we do the visualisation we need to find a way of doing it that supports our not being distracted. When you are singing the song to *Machig Labdron* if you feel lonely and sad you can sing it as if you were a small child of three who has lost her mother and sing with a very broken heart, broken voice. You can imagine your death coming to meet you and you have to go all alone with no one there with you, and so the presence of *Machig* is very reassuring. Use the whole range of your feelings to deepen the practice.

Generally speaking it is very helpful to feel desperate when you pray. If you remember your own actual situation in *samsara* then desperation should come easily. Complacency is a big obstacle in *dharma*. But comforting words are not enough – only your own experience makes a difference. Devotion transforms the tensions of anxiety which are embedded in the energetic system of our channels and winds into a free flowing excitement as the winds collect at the navel chakra and enter the central channel, allowing dissolution in space. As with orgasmic release the greater the arousal and its preceding tension and the greater the focus of attention, the greater the impact of release and the subsequent period of void.

Prayer is not a cosmetic, it is a method for transforming yourself and the more you can be in touch with your own lostness and your fear and your anxiety the more you open to the possibility of moving through that. When we pray like that we want to have her as our sole focus of attention. If you like you can just imagine the rays of light have purified everything so everything is pure. Only two things now exist ourselves and her, with a lot of energy between us.

Then *Machig Labdron* slowly comes to the top of your head. She is very full of energy. You are also full of energy. She starts to get smaller and smaller from the feet up and the head down until turning in on herself she becomes a small ball of light. This is less elaborate manifestation as a thigle, a radiant empty sphere, the energy of the *dharmakaya*. The ball then comes down through the top of your head into your heart. Your body also turns in, collapsing down into the ball of light. So light is flowing into light. Your attention is now not on this ball of light as something apart from you because the only thing that is there is this ball of light. So your attention and the ball of light are fused in the same point and you are just in this and then this is getting smaller and smaller and smaller. As it gets smaller and smaller you feel very strange because what is happening is radically other. It is different from all usual experience. This is the ground nature.

When thoughts arise and we have the sense that we are thinking the thought, the thinker and the thought have the same ground. If we relax, our awareness is merged in the ground so that we are aware of "Oh, I am thinking, this is the thought I am thinking but I am not the I who is thinking." This arises in a state of clarity free of reification. That is it is a direct experience that words cannot really convey – it is not constructed out of concepts. Clearly it is not that you cease to have a sense of self. But having a sense of self is one of the aspects of arising. But you now have an awareness which is merged into the ground of that arising. So at the end of the meditation you can get up and walk about. But where are you walking about? Who is the one who is doing the walking?

ཨ༝

ཨྂ༔

Don Sal Melong

– GET THE POINT –

ལོག་ན་མེད་དོ་རང་གི་རྟོག༔

རང་སེམས་ཀུན་བཟང་རང་ཞལ་མཐོལ༔

མ་རྟོགས་ལོག་རྟོགས་རང་གར་འཁྲུལ༔

འཁྲུལ་རྟོག་གང་ཤར་བདག་ཏུ་བཟུང༔

*"There is no other way but to under-
stand yourself. Recognising your mind
as Samantabhadra you will see your
own face. If this is not directly experienced you will be confused by wrong
thoughts and will identify yourself with
whatever confused thoughts arise."*

All *dharma* teachings point towards awakening from ignorance. The most direct method of this is to directly experience
ones own natural condition. Whether by slow or quick paths this
is the nature of enlightenment. So the text underlines that this is

ings as separate, autonomous entities. When this second stage of ignorance is in place the mind has a lot of things to attend to and so can be busy life after life, unaware of the generation of *karma*. What seems to be clarity in *samsara* – knowledge of things, of their details and differences – is in fact a further clouding over of the one doorway to awakening. Yet none of these 'things' has ever been born; like reflections in the mirror, like a mirage, they are there and not there at the same time. Empty arisings have no power – it is the mind, our minds that get lost, mistaking what is actually the case.

২৩

ཀྱི༔

Don Sal Melong

– JUST A PINBALL –

སྣང་བས་སྣང་བ་ཕྱི་ཡི་ཡུལ༔

དེ་ལ་དཔྱོད་པས་བདག་གིར་བཟུང༔

རྣམ་རྟོག་འགྱུ་འཕྲོ་ཕྲ་རགས་ལས༔

གང་ཤར་གང་དྲན་རྗེས་སུ་འབྲང༔

"Whatever appears is taken to be a variety of external objects. These are then evaluated and held to be truly existing. Subtle and insistent thoughts keep occurring and we follow after whatever arises, whatever we recollect."

Our sense of self, of being I and me, is loud with values, with memories, with likes and dislikes. When arisings are perceived they are taken to carry their own values. If we don't like fish we feel 'fish are horrible' – the fact that other people like to eat fish doesn't influence our felt experience of distaste. We experience the negative quality to be residing in the object we do not like. Inhabiting a complex world of myriad objects we make judgements without cease. With all objects ascribed valencies that can change with our mood, health, busyness etc. our minds are busy running over past events, trying to sort them out, to make sense of what has occurred. From this we develop prejudice, assumptions, hopes and fears. And we look to the future, making plans, trying to protect our interests by seeing how things might develop. But of course we don't see clearly that we are not as rational as we think we are. We don't see that what we experience as perception is largely projection and interpretation. We are not even aware of the background noise of the mind, of the continuous flow of thoughts and fantasies.

Most of the time we are fused with our mental arising, but we don't recognise it. Caught up in states of distraction we rely on the automatic pilot functions of our brain to keep us safe. While walking, driving and so on while we are miles away, caught up in an ego day dream. Only when we try to meditate do we recognise just how little control we have over what we call 'myself'. I am clearly not the one doing me. 'I' am swept along by thoughts, feelings, sensations which I only, and then but partially, recognise after the fact, after they have led me where they were going.

In the jungle of *samsara* arisings are ceaseless, there is never any let up in the interplay between past, present and future and in the turbulent interchange between inner thoughts and outer events. 'I', 'me' and 'mine' are tossed about like corks in the waves. There is no exit from this on the level of 'I'. There is no way to think yourself out of *samsara*. Even the thoughts that everything is empty, or is Padmasambhava, or pure from the very beginning do not help for no thought can unlock the door to awakening. The key is not shaped like a thing; it is not a thought, a feeling or a sensation. It's not something outer or inner. The key is your own nature, how you have been from the very beginning, simple, raw, naked, uncontrived, free of all constructs.

རྃ

ཀྵྃ

– THE FAULT OF FOCUSING ON OBJECTS –

Don Sal Melong

བཁྲུལ་བས་འཁྲུལ་བ་རྩ་གཅད་བཅད༔

མེད་པ་ལ་ཡང་ཡོད་པར་བཟུང༔

རྟགས་ཚམ་རྟོགས་ན་ཆེད་དུ་འཛིན༔

དེ་དག་ཉམས་ལེན་མ་ཡིན་ཏེ༔

བསྒོམ་གྱི་གནད་མཆོང་མཐོང་བ་མིན༔

"*Some people try to make use of confusion to cut the root of confusion. They believe in the existence of that which does not exist and think that an understanding of the signification of the objects is very important. This is not the way to do practice, this is the way not to see the faults in your meditation.*"

This is a little bit technical. When people try to make use of confusion to end confusion they are using the methods of *samsara* to get out of *samsara* The thinker and the thought are born together, by thinking about thinking which involves relying on thoughts it is impossible to free oneself from the power of thoughts. It is like drinking salt water when you are thirsty. You get some momentary relief but soon the salt starts to make your thirst worse. The answer does not lie in the fruits of confusion, therefore look to the mind not to the objects arising for/in the mind. If you focus on liberating objects, objects are ceaseless and you will have ceaseless work to do in making sure that you are liberating objects. But if you keep the focus of attention on your own awareness then by staying in the practice, by staying very closely just on the one who is doing the knowing or the thinking or the dreaming or whatever it is, all objects will automatically liberate themselves and the line of continuity of awareness will never be broken.

When we lose the direct connection of awareness, we become involved in many thoughts and feelings and these are endless They seem to be coming from all directions, they come at us, over us, behind us, out of us. So clearly, what will happen in our med-itation and in our ordinary life is that we will lose the sense of awareness and we will get lost in the many, many things of our ordinary existence. If we then try to sort out all the objects that are arising we will be very, very busy. A small child who has lost its mother in a big department store will run anxiously to each person "mama, mama, mama", and get more and more excited and confused as its energy is cooking up. The child in its anxiety has lost confidence in its mothers ability to find it. But in this *nyingma* practice we have great belief in the mother, in the nature of our own mind, and if we loose our awareness all we have to do is to be very calm and the thread of awareness will again arise and find us without any need for hysterical activity.

If you are depressed even if you are suicidal you don't need to go to a psychiatrist, you don't need to sort out any problems, you just need to focus your attention on the one who is being sui-cidal. If you are very anxious and have panic attacks and think you are going to collapse in the street you again don't need to go to a psychologist. All you have to do is: stay with the one who is feeling anxious. At all times and in all situations do not abandon yourself.

The key instruction is do not chase after objects. Relax. Relax into the out breath. Do this again and again. Thoughts, objects, impulses will arise and pass. If they appear to stay, to dominate and control you then relax further. Do not go along with the object, do not struggle to resist the object. Just relax and return to the experience of instant presence, presence which is there always, which does not need to be constructed or developed.

Of course this is difficult. When we are so addicted to objects, when we rely on coffee to lift us up, alcohol to sooth us, possessions to reassure us, etc., etc., then it is very unsettling to let go of object reliance and to focus on the unborn awareness. To do this is the basis of liberation. When, due to the power of causes and conditions, we are unable to do this then we need to use suitable antidotes from *dharma* and from banks, psychiatrists, supermarkets etc. It is foolish to image that one is in the state of *dzogchen* when one is merely confused. But for yogis it is important to keep faith with the teaching and the practice and not fall under the sway of the instant gratification of objects. Consciousness and awareness are not the same. Practice in good times when you are happy so that when tears come you will, from your own experience, know that awareness not object focused consciousness is the real refuge.

In principle there is no reason why this meditation should ever end since the natural state is there without effort. Our awareness of it only ends when we start to make effort. So stop making effort, trust, relax and effortlessly awareness will be present.

ༀ

VERSE 25

– THE GREAT COMPLETION –

དོན་ལ་རྣམ་རྟོག་ཤར་བ་མ་བཅོས་ཀློད༔

གང་ཤར་རོ་བོ་བསྐྱང་བའི་སེམས་ཉིད་འདི༔

མ་འོངས་སྐྱོན་བསུ་བདས་པའི་རྗེས་མི་གཅོད༔

ད་ལྟའི་ཤེས་པ་ཀ་དག་སོ་མའི་ངང༔

"When thoughts about the immutable nature arise, remain relaxed without doing anything artificial. Mind itself abides in its own nature whatever arises. Neither wait expectantly for what might come nor seek to follow what has gone. Abide in the ever-fresh state of the primordially pure present awareness."

"When thoughts about the immutable nature arise, remain relaxed without doing anything artificial." Thoughts about the immutable nature mean any of the ordinary dualistic thoughts we have. It does not mean that you are particularly thinking "Oh, now I am a Buddhist, now I am a meditator. What thoughts do I have about my own nature?" Thoughts that arise are always connected with the immutable nature. They have no other source. *Dharma* thoughts may be holy but they are holy thoughts and thoughts are not good if someone relies on them too much. *Dharma* thoughts can tie you up just as much as worldly thoughts. Because the imprisoning effect of the thought is not a quality of the content of the thought, that is to say what it is actually manifesting, but it is a quality of the underlining structure of the way we usually experience thoughts. Therefore whether you have holy thoughts that will take you up to heaven or terrible thoughts that will take you down to hell you have to deal with them in the same way. And that is just to remain relaxed without doing anything artificial.

"Mind itself abides in its own nature whatever arises." If we can see that the mind stays in its own state whatever arises, then no matter what arises there will be no disturbance to this natural state. As Rigdzin Godem says in the prayer *Mi rTag rGyud bsKul – Encouragement on Impermanence*: "The mind is not made by good thoughts and it is not destroyed by bad thoughts." Buddhahood, enlightenment is not created by lots of good thoughts nor is it lost by lots of bad thoughts. This path is called *dzogpa chenpo (rDzogs Pa Chhen Po)* which means the great completion or perfectly full. That is to say the state of presence is such that it doesn't require anything to improve it. And because of that the normal intentions that we have of trying to avoid situations that will destroy our good situation, and of trying to add extra thoughts, feelings and situations that will improve our good situation, can be let go of. Our ordinary self, our ego self is a point arising from the nature of the mind. It is not the nature of the mind itself. The ego needs clothes while awareness, this natural awareness, is completely naked.

"Neither wait expectantly for what might come nor seek to follow what has gone. Abide in the ever-fresh state of the primordially pure present awareness." At first we try to do this when we are sitting on our meditation seat in order to develop our clarity. But the goal is to be able to take this view into ordinary activity in the world. By avoiding distraction into the past or future we remain with a phenomenological attention, being present with whatever is arising. This permits very precise responsiveness to life as it unfolds. Rather than enacting *karmic* impulses and habitual reactivity, responsiveness is fresh and co-emergent with field of experience. This spontaneity is referred to as *'lhundrup' (Lhun Grub)* or 'effortlessly arising' or 'miraculously occurring'. Through trusting that openness will provide a response for each moment there is less and less tension to feed ego's anxious scanning of the future and rigid defensive application of old assumptions.

For example, here in our camp when you go to have your food, the food is available in big pots and you put some on your plate. You make a decision about how much food to put on your plate. If you are not going to starve you have to eat something. Somehow food has to go onto your plate. How you can take the mood of the meditation into the simple process of putting food on your plate? The easiest way is simply to be living in your own body because then you know what your hunger is. Your hunger will tell you how much food to put on your plate. And that is how we can be all the time in every situation. The more attention we have which is actually connected to the field of arising the more fine tuned our responses will be. But if we are not in our body our food will be chosen not by our felt need but by our thoughts and feelings, so we may have an image of an ideal weight and in striving to fit that representation we become anorexic. Or we may eat in order to displace an emotional need, a yearning for love, or a deep fear, and then we become bulemic.

If the four basic activities of walking, sitting, eating and sleeping are performed with a simple amount of basic awareness then its easy. When you walk you don't fall over. When you sit you don't jump about. When you eat you are not starving or stuffed. When you sleep you are sleeping and there is some awareness in the sleep. Between birth and death the demands placed on us are not very great. We ourselves place many demands on ourselves due to the constructions of our own concepts and thinking: 'I should look like this' or 'I should be like that', 'I need to please these people.' We make many, many additional activities, all of which generate *karma*.

༢༦

ཨཱོཾ

116

Don Sal Melong

– ABIDE NATURALLY –

བར་སྣང་རླུང་དང་རི་གཟར་འབབ་ཆུ་བཞིན༔

འཁྲུལ་བའི་རྣམ་རྟོག་བཀག་པས་མི་ཐུབ་ཅིང༔

ཅི་ཤར་གང་ཤར་རིག་སྟོང་རོ་བོ་སྐྱོངས༔

> *"The flow of confusing thoughts can-
> not be stopped, just like the wind or a
> waterfall in the mountains. Therefore
> towards whatever arises, however it
> arises maintain the natural state of
> open awareness."*

"The flow of confusing thoughts cannot be stopped, just like the wind or a waterfall in the mountains." One of the great mistakes that can be made in meditation is to misunderstand the meaning of calmness and tranquillity. If calmness is seen as the absence of thoughts then one will be abiding in a state where nothing is going on – a quiescence of arisings. This is the highest state in *samsara*, the most refined formless meditation – but it is in *samsara,* and when the causes that created this situation are exhausted the yogi will again be confronted with thoughts and experiences and will have a rude awakening to his limitations. Thoughts are not the enemy, objects are not the enemy. The problem lies not in arisings per se but in our attachments to them as real, separate entities. The mind has two aspects, stillness and movement, one is not better than the other; presence in both is required. Arisings, thoughts, feelings, sensations cannot be stopped. Control is a misleading fantasy. Again this is counter-intuitive to the ego. For the survival of its own sense of great importance, and for the maintainance of the messages it has learned at home and at school and in life, the ego, our egos, feel the need to control what is going on. This is a key falsity, a key point of going astray – to imagine that what cannot be controlled can be controlled.

The task is to maintain the presence of awareness, to abide in an openness that welcomes all arisings, and is without hopes or fears towards them. For the particular interest, in terms of *dzogchen,* is not what is arising but how it is liberated. Without clinging, without grasping, without going back trying to sort out bad things from the past, without going forward trying to control the world, we just stay relaxed and open and try to let each moment pass freely without attachment so that there is again fresh space for the next moment. If you are going to have an ordinary life limitation will be part of it. If you have a job and you have to be at your job on time, the watch that you live by and the diary that you live by are not the enemy. The watch is not an attack on freedom. It is just something arising. If you make a life with someone or if you make babies with someone there are duties and responsibilities that should be carried out. These duties are not the enemy of *dzogchen.*

The text says: "Therefore towards whatever arises, however it arises maintain the natural state of open awareness." This means that we have to develop a very big stomach so that we can digest the whole of our lives. We don't want to be like picky eaters, taking some things off the plate and trying to leave others. Of course we have to make choices. But the one who makes the choice is a responsive arising whose nature is awareness. If ego controls our subjectivity choices will be defensive and indulgent.

But if subjectivity is integrated into open awareness then choices will be light, not over invested with the false belief that the answer lies in the object. So we live with our eyes open and our ears open and our hearts open and accept the shape that our lives are in. If we do this then the ordinary situation will reveal itself as the natural radiance of the mind.

རབ

VERSE 27

རབ

119

– CONFUSION RESOLVES ITSELF –

Confusion Resolves Itself

བཁྲལ་བ་མེད་པར་རང་ས་ཞེན་པའི་ཚེ༔

དཔེར་ན་ཆུ་བོའི་རྒྱ་མཚོར་རྒྱུག་པ་བཞིན༔

རང་སར་ཞིག་བཞིན་བློ་ཡིས་མ་བཙལ་བར༔

"When one can abide in one's own place free of confusion it is like a river flowing back into the ocean. Thoughts subside in their own place so there is no need to seek smart solutions."

If we have a body there will always be problems with the body. If we have a relationship there will always be problems in relationship. If you try to do anything at all in your life there will always be some difficulties. That is how things are. So we should not be surprised that it is that way. The text says: "Thoughts subside in their own place so there is no need to seek smart solutions." All the *lamas* who I have ever met have had problems in their lives. They have problems in their relationships, problems with their students, problems with their own children. But the key thing is how they are able to live with these problems. They don't deny that the problems are there but they don't make a big thing of them because problems are normal. We should not be surprised that we have problems.

The one solution to all problems is to abide in ones own place and trust that all arising things are passing things. All manifestation is impermanent. It is attachment, desire and impatience that have us seeking for special solutions, answers that will let us live life on our terms. But these short term solutions bring no real freedom for they wind us further and further into reified duality. All manifestation, whether 'good' or 'bad' arises from the open ground nature and returns to it.

Our usual sense is that thoughts lead somewhere. Even when we have very unproductive forms of thinking, like habitual worrying, it is normal for us to believe that going over the same issues again and again will somehow provide some new insight. Now instead of following the content, which seems so fascinating, if we focus on the manner of thinking we see that we have to think again about something because the first thought we had has gone, and now so has the second, and so on. Repeated thoughts keep the object/image alive for us, as if it was selfexisting rather than being the by-product of the stream of thoughts. Each thought has to be replaced by another because they keep vanishing. They are impermanent – without the least effort on our part they vanish by themselves. This is the self-liberation of thinking – and by extension of the same principle we can experience the self-liberation of all ideas, all arisings. It is ego's work of recycling ideas, of repetition compulsion, of restaging, transference etc. etc. that creates the illusion of the ongoing existence of that which is momentary.

Lived experience of this, and especially lived experience of the impermanent nature of all the arisings out of which we construct our sense of self, allows a letting go so that movement can arise and pass revealing the stillness that never changes. This stillness is the ground nature of the mind, ungraspable, not an object or a thing, unblemished by any arising it is relaxed, open, undefended and welcoming to all arisings as they come and go.

ॐ

VERSE 28

– ALWAYS ALREADY PRESENT –

གཞི་མེད་རྩ་བྲལ་གནས་ལུགས་རང་བཞིན་སྟོང་ༀ

གསལ་སྟོང་ཟུང་འཇུག་ལྷ་མ་བཅོས་པའི་ག་ལའི་གཤིསༀ

"Without a ground (ignorance), devoid of any root (kleshas) the natural condition is of itself empty. Clarity and emptiness are merged as the non-artificial quality of awareness."

This verse again points out that the natural state has no grasping roots or substantial ground. It has no basis, no self-existence as an entity and because of this, clarity or illumination and emptiness are merged in the very process of noetic being.

Now clearly Nuden Dorje has already stated this several times but he repeats it again from slightly different points of view to really clarify the key issue that if your point of activity, your sense of yourself as you move into relationship with the world, appears to be resting on something, that is a sign that you are already trapped.

The purpose of the teaching is to give you confidence to trust that the mind is pure from the beginning. You cannot purify that which is already pure so don't waste time in that direction. That which is always pure is beyond defilement so drop your guilty anxieties about being full of ignorance and sin. Practice relaxation into the natural condition and experience the self liberation of all arisings. Then there is nothing to be purified and manifestation is revealed as the natural clarity of the mind, precise, detailed and empty.

ཟླ

ཟླ

– GIVE IT A REST –

Give it a Rest

གང་ཤར་རོ་བོ་བསྐྱང་བར་འཛིན་མེད་གློད༔

གནས་ན་ཁྱུན་ཅིང་བསྒོམ་ཏུ་མ་ཡིན་ཏེ༔

གཉིས་དང་འཕོ་དང་དགག་སྒྲུབ་མེད་པར་སྐྱོང༔

"Keeping to the nature of whatever arises there is relaxation free of grasping. If your mind becomes steady you don't have to maintain this with meditation. Remain free of encouraging or inhibiting, stability or movement."

The first line of this verse points out that attention to the impermanence of arisings brings with it relaxation in the observer. The more you see there is nothing for you to do the more you find yourself relaxing. This leads to the second line for with relaxation there is a centering in openness, a feeling of spaciousness, an unwavering sense of presence, undisturbed by changes in the flow of arisings and therefore effortful forms of meditation are not required. So the third line says don't take up with the flow of experience – controlling self, controlling other, these methods lead only to confusion.

Garab Dorje set out the basics of *dzogchen* in his famous three statements:

> Direct recognition of one's own nature.
> Not remaining in doubt.
> Continuing in confidence.

Each statement provides an orientation for meditation. In simple terms if you imagine you have a bicycle and you are trying to learn to ride it. The kind of movements that you make when you first get on it are designed to stop you falling over, but they are usually agitated and it takes a while to recognise how to balance. Once you can ride a bicycle you are still making subtle adjustments with your body weight, pressure of the pedals and steering, in order to keep the bicycle upright and this is like the work of learning how to get back in balance. With this you start to trust that you can maintain balance and so give up the doubt and anxious tightening that causes you to wobble. Then we develop the confidence to maintain balance even in heavy traffic or over rough countryside.

As we try at first to get on the bicycle or to have the direct experience of the mind it is quite difficult because we can't find the point of balance, of relaxation. The bicycle keeps falling over and we say: "Why does it not stay up?" and we get on it again but are off balance and so then it falls over. We begin the meditation already off balance, off balance in terms of our energy, off balance in terms of our assumptions, off balance in terms of our motivation and this stops us relaxing into the sense of balance.

We can use this metaphor in relation to the four points mentioned in the text: encouraging and inhibiting, stability and movement. If you are trying to get on the bicycle and you encourage one side too much, if you push too hard one way, that knocks you off balance. And if you try to block a wobble by applying the brakes you will not get in balance. The same applies with stability, if you try to hold the bicycle steady and just rest on it you will fall over. If you go too much into move-

Don Sal Melong

ment you will veer about and lose your poise. If you can remember learning to ride a bicycle or learning to swim you will recall that at a certain point you found yourself just doing it and that point is inseparable from relaxation. I think it is a very important point because if you are trying to recognise the nature of your mind at first you do it very busily. You are trying to do something. If you are lucky you will get tired, do less, and there will be a bit more space and then suddenly you find yourself. It is about not letting go so loosely that you lose all awareness but also not getting so tight that you push against yourself. There is no magic way. No one can do it for you. But by relaxing, observing yourself, seeing how you are conditioned and practicing gently and tenderly one day you will find you are in the groove and there it is.

ग़ुर

Give it a Rest

༻༠

ཨྃ༔
ༀ

126

– THE CHAIN OF THOUGHTS –

ཤར་བའི་དུས་ན་གཅིག་གྲོགས་གཅིག་གིས་བྱེད༔

གྲོལ་བའི་དུས་ན་མཉམ་གྲོལ་ཆོས་ཉིད་ཀློང༔

ཆོས་ཀུན་སྟེང་པོ་མཐར་ཐུག་དེ་ཁོ་ན༔

*"At the time of arising thoughts sup-
port each other like a chain of friends.
At the time of dissolving they dissolve
evenly in the vastness of openness. The
ultimate nature of all phenomena is
simply this."*

When thoughts are arising, the text says they "support each
other like a chain of friends." In old village style if somebody's house
is on fire everybody rushes there with their buckets and the buckets
are passed up the line. Somebody is filling the bucket and somebody
is throwing it on the house but everybody is involved in the chain.
That is to say the linked activity of the arising thoughts carries a sense
of intentionality and purpose. Then when the purpose, which

seemed so vital, is fulfiled the chain dissolves. "At the time of dissolving they dissolve evenly in the vastness of openness." Each thought in turn vanishes into openness. No matter what impact they made as they arose each vanishes in the same way.

"The ultimate nature of all phenomena is simply this." One thought by itself has no meaning. Thoughts need to rest on each other to create the structures of meaning. This is the traditional Buddhist idea of dependent co-origination. If in meditation you find that one thought leads to another you should not be surprised. That's what thoughts do. Thoughts have an automatic tendency to built up structures of meaning together. But they are each of them devoid of any inherent reality and so the structures that they built up are also devoid of inherent reality. And that is what we experienced when we used the syllable 'Phat'. We use the 'Phat' to cut a hole in the line of thoughts so there is a gap. Now after you say the 'Phat' thoughts come back. But imagine if thoughts didn't come back. What would you do?

Thoughts are not the problem. It is our grasping, investing relationship with thoughts that creates the problem. Thoughts are simply a mode of manifestation of the natural energy of the mind. In a traditional example the *dharmakaya* is like the sun, the *sambhogakaya* is like the radiance of the sun, and the *nirmanakaya* is like a ray of light that carries heat and light with it.

The key thing is to recognise that all the experiences one is having are just the natural radiance of the mind. Even if we have thoughts such as: "I am a terrible person, I am unable to love, I am unlovable," these thoughts are also the natural radiance of the mind. And if we have the thoughts, "I am a very wonderful person and I am entitled to a great deal of love and respect and money from everybody else," that thought is also the natural radiance of the mind. This is very, very important. Because if you believe some thoughts are good and some thoughts are bad then you are condemning yourself to eternity in *samsara*. Thoughts are neither good nor bad in themselves – it is the egos attribution of value that creates seemingly innate differences. Of course in relative truth good and bad exist but they exist relatively. You cannot have good without having bad. They complement each other. These distinctions have no absolute truth but if we are going to be with human beings it is better if we are kind and helpful and thoughtful rather than selfish and greedy.

༣༡

ཨོཾ

128

– ILLUSION AND ETHICS –

ཚོགས་དྲུག་སྣང་བ་བསླུ་བས་རྗེས་མ་འབྲང༔
སྤྱོད་ལམ་རྣམས་དང་ཉིད་མཚན་བཟོར་ཡུག་ཏུ༔
བྱ་བྱེད་འཁྲུལ་བ་རྨི་ལམ་སྒྱུ་མ་བཞིན༔

"Don't pursue the deceitful phenome-
na which appear through the six senses.
During the day or night, whatever activ-
ity you engage in, the notion of a doer
and a deed is just a confusing illusion,
like a dream or magic."

Many different kinds of appearances come to us through
the six senses. There are the consciousnesses linked to the five
sense organs and the mental consciousness which processes the
results of sense experience and these are described as manifesting deceitful phenomena. In *tantra* when we take refuge in the
guru we try to rely as much as possible on him because there is a
sense that he doesn't cheat, that he is directly in relation with

something meaningful. Whereas the phenomena that arise through our own self experience are usually quite deceptive and deceitful.

It does not really matter if experiences are 'true' or 'false' in themselves, the main reason that these phenomena are described as deceitful is that they cover over the possibility of recognising the nature of your mind. As we saw previously, it is not that they are other than your mind for they are the energetic manifestation of the nature of your mind. But because we see them as if they were something truly separate they deceive us. Some of you may know the paintings of René Magrite. He has one where there is a very simple painting of a pipe and it says 'This is not a pipe'. The phenomena that arise in our minds do not really exist. So that instead of there being a pipe and a statement 'This is not a pipe', actually there is no pipe but the statement is 'This is a pipe' or 'This is my life' or 'These are my feet' or 'This is my watch'. It is like when we point to our image in a mirror and say 'this is me' – but it is only a reflection in an empty mirror. So what is important is that the deceitful nature of these phenomena is not inherent in the phenomena. The deceit arises from our relationship to them. Because again if they were truly deceitful we would have to avoid them forever in order to be safe and if we had to do that we would be acting into a split between *samsara* and *nirvana*.

"During the day or the night, whatever activity you engage in, the notion of a doer and a deed is just a confusing illusion, like a dream or magic." This is very interesting because it brings us to one of the most problematic dimensions of *dzogchen* which is that of ethics. Because what are the actual implications for ordinary life if you say that the notion of a doer and a deed is just a confusing notion, an illusion?

On one level everything that arises is an illusion. That is to say it is devoid of inherent existence. At the same time when a dog comes and shits just outside the door somebody has got to clean it because although the nature of the shit is illusion if it sticks on your foot it is a smelly illusion on your own dear foot. So how can you clear up the dog shit and do the dishes and help your children with their homework and get to work on time, how can you do that within the view of *dzogchen*? If we have rich sponsors or parents who will subsidise us, practice is reasonably easy. But for many people here practising the *dharma* involves real sacrifices. It means other people are not getting the attention they want, money is being lost, there is pressure from the world. It is very important to have respect for the nature of our shared *karmic* experience which is this aspect or this dimension of being human beings at this time. All our actions have consequences and if the immediate effects of our actions have to be borne by other people so that we are able to practice the *dharma* that is something to be aware of. Because although we may be trying to stay with the illusory nature of the doer and the deed, how we are in the world is also visible to other people and they don't share this notion that it is an illusion. So there is some tension here between wisdom and compassion. We could see compassion as taking other peoples thoughts and feelings seriously, or from a 'higher' view we could see compassion as the realisation that they are trapped in their limiting assumptions and therefore we should act so as not to confirm these assumptions.

In Tibet there were monks and nuns and lay people and yogis, each with different ways of practising the *dharma*. Each of these styles of *dharma* practice had particular cultural traditions and were manifesting according to certain clear principles. Monks and nuns have vows. Vows of poverty and vows of chastity and these should always be respected. Maintaining any kind of vow in our modern time is very hard and if we put pressure on other people to break their vows that is generally unhelpful. Vows that have been kept for ten, fifteen years can be broken with just one smile. Another *dharma* style is that of people who decide to live the life of a yogi. This carries very powerful commitments for in taking the initiation seriously you enter into the sacred space of the mandala. This means that the sense of the whole world as sacred has to be maintained all the time. Which means not harming people, not exploiting them, not being self indulging. If you choose to take that path then you need to learn what the *tantric* vows really are and keep them. Otherwise you might feel you can just ceaselessly define whatever you do and whatever you want as pure and holy but the one who is doing that is likely to be your ego.

All human learning comes in a lineage. Our parents pass on to us what they have learned as do school teachers. So do friends in the play ground. The friend who gives us our first cigarette and shows us how to smoke is also part of a lineage, a transmission. Learning from books involves skills we have learnt at school. We are always in relation to others. Therefore respect and gratitude to all teachers is important, even if they taught us badly, or taught us bad things – for what they were demonstrating is the inseparability of self and other. We internalise what was externalised by others, and in turn we externalise to others what we have internalised. This pulsation weaves the co-emergence of inner and outer, subject and object, self and other, giving and receiving. Each knowledge carries a sense of how it is to be used. For esoteric learning, such as *tantra* and *dzogchen*, it is vital to have a living transmission from someone who has received not just the teaching but the permission to teach. Very often teachers only empower one or two of their students to teach for the lineage needs living integration of the view, meditation, activity and result if it is to carry its full force.

In Tibet there was a very traditional culture that maintained hierarchy with a very clear choreography of social positions and roles. Here in the west we have a very different culture. In Tibet *lamas* were rarely questioned, there was very little confronting of powerful people about their behaviour. Here in the west we are all accountable. The kind of behaviour that we will tolerate from teachers is very different from that in Tibet. So we have some extra problems, problems that highlight the complex relation between relative and absolute truth. On the one hand in order to do practice we need to believe the *guru* is a buddha, on the other hand, in order to be on the right side of our tax system, we need to ensure that money collected for religious purposes such as monastery building is actually spent on that. But who has the right and/or the power to enquire into this? These are real problems – the conflict between the meditationally useful power of idealisation and the ethically necessary power to hold people accountable. *Dharma* in the west requires both teachers and students to behave in different ways. Since mistakes are inevitable apology from both sides should not be too difficult, surely?

In the traditional formulation, wisdom should be as vast as the sky and compassion should be as fine as the point of a needle. The three modes of nature: open, radiant, responsive operate together so that there is no privileging of self over other. Sensitivity, tenderness, empathy are aspects of responsiveness. They are kept free of need and attachment through their emergence from radiance which has the aspects of clarity, spontaneity and dynamism. And radiance is kept free of inflation and self-reference through its emergence from openness which has the aspects of purity, satisfaction, and changelessness. The integrated flow of these modes brings ethics into each moment of life. Objectification, assumption, appropriation, exploitation etc., etc. are self-liberate before they can ensnare both self and other.

How we are energetically impacts others, our happiness, our sadness, our hopelessness, our faith. This is an inescapable aspect of co-emergence. Therefore the integration of our experience in the three modes described above is the best way of making the most precious of offerings, the offering of openness.

It is easy to get lost. I myself clearly get lost a great deal of the time. I find myself doing things that upset other people, things that I regret doing. There is the on-going difficulty of trying to maintain the state of openness in which guilt and shame and concern about my own actions can be lightened and loosened up so that they do not become a heavy force for the next moment and the need to respond to the impact of my actions on others.

Just as we do *Dorje Sempa* confession and purification practice many times in the *Big Rigdzin* practice, we can take this view into the personal dimension and apologise to people for mistakes we have made and for things that we have done that have upset them. It's not about making long explanations and justifications of why we did what we did but to be sincerely aware that living in the state of unawareness as we do, we hurt other people. It is not just that hurting people is bad because they are like us and we ourselves don't like to suffer. But energetically when we get upset, when we feel angry with someone, when we feel put down or ignored or somebody does something that makes us jealous, we shrink, we become tight, we are not at ease. So whether this tension is arising in ourselves or in others it impacts on all those around and if this influences peoples ability to collaborate as a *Sangha*, to practice together it is very unhelpful. The best remedy is to practice *Guru Yoga* together.

From the very beginning of beginningless *samsara* we have been engaged in the activity of ignorance and we have accumulated the five poisons and done many, many things to hurt and harm others. So it is predictable that we will continue to do things that upset and hurt other people. But the task in *dzogchen* is to go deeply into open awareness and to develop clarity, and responsiveness, an energetic engagement with the world that reveals itself as it is. From time to time we develop fantasies about people, loving fantasies on the basis of which we say things to them, giving them reasons to believe in us or hope for things and then our mind changes and we betray the shared fantasy, the folie à deux. There are no self-existing objects. Projecting onto others is projecting onto projections. Bearing that in mind keeps things light so that situations, even if painful, can be resolved. The answer lies in us, not in the other. Relaxing, keeping loose, light and responsive supports our entering instant presence in the midst of life's complexity.

This is not a Buddha

Homage to René Magrite

ༀༀ

VERSE 32

– AWARENESS, AWARENESS, AWARENESS –

Don Sal Melong

སྣང་ཚོས་མ་འགགས་རྡོན་ལ་སྒྲུབ་པ་མེད༔

གང་ཤར་རྩིས་གདབ་མེད་བཞིན་མཐའ་བྲལ་བློ༔

དུས་དང་རྣམས་པ་ཀུན་ཏུ་དྲན་རིག་དང་༔

*"Don't try to block appearances, they
are devoid of substantial reality.
Towards whatever arises maintain an
attitude free of limitation, without
judgement or prejudice. At all times
and in all situations maintain the state
of alert awareness."*

"**D**on't try to block appearances, they are devoid of substantial reality." We allow whatever is coming to us to come.
Clearly that doesn't mean that we should intentionally put ourselves in danger, that we should be unaware and get into trouble.
It doesn't mean that. Parents have to look after children because
children are not aware. Awareness is a very good protection.

People who practice awareness should not be making too many mistakes. Problems of course come but there is a sense of being very much in contact with the field of manifestation. Through this one is able to respond in the situation without over reacting to it. Not to block appearances means to maintain absolute presence with the presence of the appearance. So you have a co-emergent presence. And of course one of the things that makes this kind of text very difficult to read is that when we hear the instruction "Don't try to block appearances," it is as if that instruction is coming to ourselves, to our ordinary sense of self: "Oh, I better remember not to do that." But the self who is trying not to block appearances is itself an appearance.

We and our world are appearances. This is represented by the word *nang wa (sNang Ba)* which also means light, and all visible appearance. It also, more particularly in *dzogchen*, means experience because an appearance is an experience. If it appears somebody experiences it. It appears to someone. It doesn't just appear by itself, in itself. Thus we can be present in the experience of our existence so that openness and experience are inseparable and the experiencer shows its paradoxical modality as both infinite presence and specific momentary agency. Whatever comes, comes; whatever goes, goes. Life, reality is what happens. As John Lennon said: "Life is what happens while you are busy making other plans." This is a beautiful thing to say. It is exactly true and you can spend all your time making plans to do retreats, to do meditation, to do *mantras*, to remember that you are some deity and while you are making these plans your life will go wrong in its usual ways. So the key thing is to be present in life as it occurs, which means to really be nowhere else other than in this continuum of existence which is you and the world as you experience it.

"Towards whatever arises maintain an attitude free of limitation, without judgement or prejudice. At all times and in all situations maintain the state of alert awareness." We become limited when we bring our old baggage into the situation. On the basis of *karmic* tendencies developed in previous lives and patterns, habits, and reactions developed in this life, we interpret experiences while thinking we are being open to them. This is a big mistake. Again and again we should relax, open, not take things too seriously and return to what is here, what is occurring in the linked domains of subject and object. Without bias, without going to either side maintain awareness of the integrated field of arising. When we find we have slipped back into primary identification with the self as subject there is no need to despair, just relax, open and allow whatever comes to come. The more we see our own specific ways of foreclosure, of sealing off, of limiting and defensively separating the more we can relax blame, and allow energy to tighten and loosen while abiding in presence.

Remember that awareness is not me being aware of something. It is not that I am aware of things, it is that within the state of awareness the felt sense of an I arises giving attention and interest to other arisings which are within the field.

ཟ‌ཟ

ཟ‌ཟ

– THE LIE OF OUR LIVES –

སྐད་ཅིག་རྒྱུས་སོ་བྱ་ར་མ་བཞག་པར༔

ཡེངས་མེད་འཛིན་མེད་མི་འདུག་སྐྱོང་བ་གནད༔

"Don't relax your alert attention for even an instant. It is vital to maintain non-distraction, non-grasping, non-avoidance."

"**D**on't relax your alert attention for even an instant. It is vital to maintain non-distraction, non-grasping, non-avoidance." There was a British psychoanalyst called Donald Winnicott who discovered that for many patients who where suffering from a great fear of having a breakdown, of going mad, the reality was that the breakdown had already occurred. Very often we turn away from things in our life because we feel they are unbearable. Because we feel that if we were to look at our actual situation, it would make us crazy, it would destroy us in some way. But truly we have all already had our breakdown. We are all quite mad. We are mad with ignorance and the five poisons. And as with any kind of madness the cure lies in looking at the relation between the symptom and its originatory cause.

The symptoms that we have are lying to ourselves, lying to others, cheating ourselves with fantasies, with denial and avoidance. And the root cause of that is the habit of ignorance which blocks us moment by moment from recognising the open dimension of being. And here is the real paradox because the doorway into the natural condition exists only in the moment. But the present moment is the one place where we find it very difficult to live. Because somehow we imagine that being caught up in thoughts of the past and thoughts about the future is healthier, more important and easier to manage than being present in what is going on now. So it is very important to hear the feeling, the affective tone of this verse because it is not an abstract cognitive proposition. It is something which when we engage with it will turn us upside down, make us very disturbed. When we try not to grasp, not to be distracted and not to avoid things, we start to face the terror of the lie that we have been living for so long.

So there is a double move here. To be relaxed while being ceaselessly attentive and to be attentive while remaining relaxed. This is similar to the stance required in martial arts. It is the middle way that avoids the extremes. The key lies in satisfaction *(Sim Pa)*, in enjoying the plenum void of presence, the fullness of being which comes with the separation and integration of stillness and movement. By not investing hopes and fears in impermanent arisings there is nothing to distract, grasp or avoid. The beginning and end of *dharma* practice is refuge. If you find the refuge of your own nature you will have no need to seek the deceiving refuge of fleeting objects.

ཞང་

VERSE 34

– BE KIND TO YOURSELF –

སྟོང་ཉིད་སྙིང་རྗེ་མ་ཡེངས་མ་བསྒོམ་པར༔

རྣམ་པ་ཀུན་ཏུ་འབད་རྩོལ་དང་བྲལ་ནས༔

མཉམ་བཞག་རྗེས་ཐོབ་རྒྱུན་ཏུ་བསམ་གཏན་བསྒོམ༔

"Maintain emptiness and compassion without distraction or striving meditation. Always free of effort and struggle contemplate the flow of meditative evenness and its subsequent effect."

The key thing is to be kind to yourself. The barriers we have to entering into presence are already hard enough. If we try to become great heroes and push our way through we will make the resistance even greater. Tenderness and love are always important. Being tender towards ourselves, being very finely attuned to what is going on is like caressing the face of a little child. We are not trying to stare into our mind but are just trying very gently to be present with whatever occurs.

If somebody comes to us and tells us that they have done terrible things and that they are upset about it, we feel touched by that and we want to help them. All the bad things that we have ever done, the things that we feel ashamed about, we have done out of the five poisons. We have done them out of our own confusion and pain.

The path to integration is not through punishment but through tenderly accepting ourselves as we are so that we can come close to ourselves. And if we come close to ourselves then the most subtle breach of subject and object as two entities is gradually collapsed. And through the moment of loving ourselves very deeply and profoundly, which is at the heart of all meditation, we make this primary integration into the ground nature. If we take up this tender attention it will take us into the depths of meditative evenness, which means the state in which the mind is not disturbed by anything at all that arises. And then it will go with us into the stage of subsequent effect, which is the post-meditative state or the expansive aspect of meditation in which we find ourselves in the world with other people. If we can be relaxed and integrate these two states, that is said to be the nature of buddhahood.

The natural condition is not against you, other people are not against you in your nature, primarily we are against ourselves. When we start to collaborate with ourselves, when we get on the same side as ourselves, the world turns around and we start to feel this flow of energy coming through us. And we start to awaken to the fact that we are nothing but this non-dual integrated manifestation of presence.

This verse marks the end of the teaching part of the text. We have now the concluding verses which are more general. But we have received the essence of this text which is a direct transmission, a *terma* transmission through Nuden Dorje, concerning the nature of the mind and the attitude to be adopted. Relaxation is not laziness and kindness to oneself is not self indulgence. As the text describes in several places the quality of awareness is clarity and presence. So if these two things are not in our experience we are probably getting lost. Be careful!

Don Sal Melong

༣༥

VERSE 35

– NOTHING BETTER THAN THIS –

དེ་ལྟར་མཛོད་པ་རྒྱུད་སྡེ་ཐམས་ཅད་ཀྱི༔

གཉིས་པའི་གནད་དོན་ཆོས་ཀྱི་སྙིང་ཁུ་བཏུད༔

བདེ་གཤེགས་རྒྱལ་བ་ཀུན་གྱི་ཉམས་ལེན་མཆོག༔

ལྟ་བསྒོམ་སྤྱོད་པའི་མན་ངག་འདི་ཡོ་ནུ༔

"This practice is the longed for essential meaning of all the classes of tantra, the vital essence of the dharma. It is the supreme practice of all the buddhas. It is the sole secret exposition of the view, meditation and conduct."

Due to Nuden Dorje's kindness we don't need to practice the whole range of *tantric* disciplines. Just to understand the key point of this text is enough. "It is the supreme practice of all the buddhas." One might think that this is a kind of hyperbole. But it is not because this is exactly the practice that the buddhas do.

It is the heart practice of the great masters like Garab Dorje and Padmasambhava. It is important to believe that it is the supreme one because one of the qualities of the dualising mind is always to have new categories with new ranges of adjectives and adverbs and always there is something higher or better. Television is full of adverbs, and superlatives setting out newer and better models. And in Tibetan Buddhism you always hear the gossip about this or that *lama* who has some very, very special teaching. So it is important to get a sense that if you do this practice you will not be cheating yourself. There is no other mystery existing anywhere else. Even if a deity has a hundred legs and a thousand arms he is not walking on any different path from this. Although this teaching is quite simple, in many ways it is exquisitely difficult to practice.

VERSE 36

– THE PROPER WAY –

སྐལ་ལྡན་ལས་འཕྲོ་ཅན་རྣམས་ཉམས་སུ་ལོངས༔

ས་དང་ལམ་གྱི་ཡོན་ཏན་གོང་དུ་འཕེལ༔

རྫོགས་པ་ཆེན་པོ་སྙིང་ཐིག་དམར་བྱུང་འདི༔

ཕྱི་རབས་ལས་ལྡན་བུ་ཡི་གྲོགས་སུ་བཅུལ༔

> *"The fortunate ones with good
> karma must do this practice then the
> good qualities of the stages and paths
> will develop and increase. This is the
> distillation of the essence of Dzogchen.
> It will be a friend to the fortunate ones
> who come later."*

𝕿hen he is saying: "The fortunate ones with good *karma* must do this practice", and if they do that all "the good qualities of the" different "stages and paths will develop…" It is a "distillation of" all "*Dzogchen*. It will be a friend to the fortunate ones who come later." The fortunate ones with good *karma* are Nuden Dorje and the first students he passed this teaching to. Through the short lineage it comes to C. R. Lama who certainly lived this text and integrated it into his life. And now through the transmission, the translation and the teaching it comes to you. So you are the fortunate ones who come later.

The teaching has to come the proper way. Never pretend you know more than you do, for to do so is not just to cheat yourself but to betray the transmission and to betray others. Only through integration does it stay alive.

It would appear from my conversations with you that most people here on retreat have rather messy lives. We are not exactly the conventional bourgeoisie. And yet we have good *karma*. And that is important. At least we have got something of real value. It is often the case that life needs to be a little fragmented for some gap or opening with the possibility of change to come into it. If there is too much comfter the practice of the *dharma* is difficult.

Don Sal Melong

ཀ

ཀ

– MAINTAIN THE LINEAGE –

Maintain the Lineage

གཏེར་སྲུང་ཚོགས་ཀྱི་བཀའ་བའི་གཉེར་ཀ་བསྲུང༌༔

དམ་ལྡན་རིགས་ལ་ལྟ་བཞིན་སྐྱོང་བ་དང༌༔

རིག་པ་ཀ་དག་ཀུན་བཟང་ཞལ་མཐོང་ཤོག༌༔

*"You protectors of the treasure doc-
trines must guard these doctrines well.
You vow-keepers must protect these
teachings as if they were your child. You
will see the face of Samantabhadra, the
primordial purity of your awareness."*

𝕿he protectors are the powerful beings who serve the *dhar-ma* by keeping an eye on what is going on. Like the super-ego they are concerned with duty, rules and punishment. Who are they going to guard these doctrines against? Clearly they don't need to protect the book against the unlucky ones who never meet it. We the lucky ones with good *karma* who have met these teachings are also the unlucky ones who are likely to threaten it by not understanding the teaching properly. We the fortunate ones who had the good *karma* to meet this teachings are also the unfortunate and unlucky ones who are likely through our own lack of attention to misunderstand and to distort the teaching. The enemies of the *dharma* are not out there. Out there are only cows and farmers. The enemies of the *dharma* are in this room, people with big egos and confused minds and lazy thinking who mix all the teachings up and pretend to themselves that they are really doing proper practice. So it is important to remember the obligation that goes with receiving teachings like these. The *dharma* is not a toy. Without respect and diligence you will only increase your suffering.

३≺

VERSE 38

३≺

– TEACHING FOR THE HEART AND NOT THE INTELLECT –

ॐ

* རྗོག་གིའི་གྲུབ་མཐའ་བ་སྐྱོད་མཁན་གྱི་རིག་གནས༔*

ཆུལ་འདི་སྟོན་པའི་དུས་མིན་རྟ་ཐེམ་རྒྱུ༔

ཤིན་ཏུ་གསང་བས་མཁའ་འགྲོའི་གསང་མཛོད་གྲགས༔

> *"It is never appropriate to show these teaching to scholars who are addicted to ratiocination and point scoring. They are sealed in emptiness. Because they are very secret they are known as the dakinis' secret treasure."*

If there is no intention to practice this teaching then there is no need to know it. When *dharma* is used to fuel intellectual egotism this is terrible. It creates an iatrogenic disorder in which the doctor and the medicine have created a new disorder. The teaching are sealed in emptiness. Only practice can penetrate emptiness. Scholars thoughts lead only to further thoughts, the endless delusions of *samsara*.

The essential point of this is that these teachings are a path of heart, that one needs one's heart open in order to practice them. As we looked earlier the way into this practice is through tenderness and with a sense of aesthetic enjoyment and aesthetic attunement as if you were listening to the Goldberg Variations. The doorway lies through energetic attunement and so they are called the dakinis' secret treasure. The dakinis respond to energy not concepts.

People with good *karma* on hearing these teachings for the first time can waken straight away. But most people need to do some preliminary practice of struggling to understand on the conceptual level the meaning of the concept. Kalu Rinpoche used to say that *tantra* was like an aeroplane. It could get you to the goal very quickly but the price of the ticket is quite high. And of course you have to buy the ticket before you can get on the plane. So you have to have accumulated some good *karma* and some mental preparation before you can engaging the practice. And the same would definitely apply to this kind of practice.

VERSE 39 & 40

– COLOPHON –

བཛྲ་མིང་གི་སྐལ་བར་གཏེར་དུ་སྦྱས༔

ཞེས་པ་འདི་བར་བདག་འདུ་ནས་ལྦན་འགྲོ་ཕན་གྱིང་པས་གངས་བཟང་གནས་ནས་
གདན་དྲངས་ཤིང་མ་ཅིག་གི་གདན་ས་ཟངས་རི་མཁར་དམར་དུ་གཏན་ལ་ཕབ་

པའོ༔

"It is hidden for the fortunate one known as Bendza Ming."

"This text was revealed by Nuden Dorje Drophan Lingpa at the holy place of Kang Zang (Gangs bZang) in North Tibet. It was written down at Machig Labdron's pilgrimage place by Zangri Khamar (Zangs Ri mKhar dMar)."

"It is hidden for the fortunate one known as Bendza Ming," that is "vajra name", which is another name of Nuden Dorje. Because the lineage is so short, so recent it has a lot of power. Still fresh it has few confused thoughts covering it. Like water from a spring it is most refreshing.

The colophon indicates that this text was written by Padmasambhava and was later discovered by Nuden Dorje in North Tibet and written down by him when he was on pilgrimage in Zangri Kharmar.

Don Sal Melong

APPENDIX

ཚོགས

Machig Labdron's Teaching
On the Nature of Wisdom

Acute people with strong faith who wish to practice the teaching of *Mahasandhi* (*Dzogchen*), should stay in a peaceful isolated place and keep all sentient beings in mind, themselves and all others.

At this time when we have the creative situation of a body having the freedoms and opportunities it is vital to meditate on the impermanence of this life. Feeling revulsion for *samsara* and developing the intention to benefit sentient beings remain calm and peaceful in body, voice and mind and meditate as follows.

The entire outer container of the world consisting of earth, stones, mountains, rocks and so on and its inner inhabitants consisting of all sentient beings are only names put by your mind. You must be really clear about this. Regarding your mind, you must again and again search for it in terms of its shape and colour, its source, resting place and destination. Whenever, due to discriminating identification, you think you have found some real self-existing essence, then test your findings by searching outside and inside, looking everywhere.

Through repeated practice and the repeated experience of finding nothing substantial, return again and again to the clarity that your mind is empty (*sunya*) and without any entitative essence whatsoever. Regarding this emptiness devoid of inherent self-substance, many different thoughts of existence and non-existence arise, yet these ideas, concepts and intellectual distinctions are themselves without substantial basis being the mere play of illusory subject and object. Without awaiting future thoughts or going after past thoughts allow the natural flow without interfering.

The awareness of the thinker, the perceiver, the understander is itself the arising of the natural expression of awareness itself. It is vital to abide always exactly in that state. It is crucial to experience whatever thoughts, feelings, sensations arise, whether pleasant or unpleasant, as the arising of the natural expression of awareness. By simply maintaining this awareness, without doing anything artificial or constructive whatsoever, liberation is the non-duality of all arisings and the wisdom of natural awareness. Integration in the state of awareness is vital.

The pristine clarity of the primordially relaxed awareness is naturally unobscured. Unwavering, it is free of substantial objects, free of attachment, shining and clear. This is the primordial ground and home of all the arisings of *samsara* and *nirvana*. Free of hopes and doubts experience your own natural awareness.

Gain the certainty that there is just this: all thoughts are inseparable from the ground nature, being the radiance of awareness. All appearances, one's own experiences, the ceaselessness of the manifestations of clarity increase and develop. Then with the actualisation of the pervasive unchanging awareness, the inexpressible nature of the inconceivable ending of phenomena, the great spontaneous non-meditation, *mahamudra*, the heart experience of *Kuntu Zangpo (Samantabhadra)* is manifest.

In the *bardo* you will be liberated in the *dharmadhatu* and will have the power to act for the benefit of all beings. This practice is vital. This concludes the introduction to the original nature of *Prajnaparamita*.

From the *Chöd* text "The vision opening the Door to Liberation (*Dag sNang Thar Pai sGo 'Byed*)" by Gonpo Wangyal (*mGon Po dBang rGyal*).

Don Sal Melong

ཨ་ཅིག་ལབ་སྒྲོན་གྱི་རྣལ་འབྱོར༔

Guru Yoga for Machig Labdron

ༀ་ཨ་ཅིག་མ་ལ་གསོལ་བ་འདེབས༔

OM MA CHIG   MA   LA   SOL WA DEB
OM* Machig Labdron   mother to   praying
OM. I pray to Machig Labdron, the mother.

ཨཱཿ ཨ་ཅིག་མ་ལ་གསོལ་བ་འདེབས༔

AA   MA CHIG   MA   LA   SOL WA DEB
AA* Machig Labdron   mother to   praying
AA. I pray to Machig Labdron, the mother.

ཧཱུྃ་ཨ་ཅིག་མ་ལ་གསོལ་བ་འདེབས༔

HUNG MA CHIG   MA   LA SOL WA DEB
HUNG* Machig Labdron   mother to praying
HUNG. I pray to Machig Labdron, the mother.

*)   Symbol of Machig Labdron's body, speech and mind.
    A white OM is on her forehead, a red AA on her throat
    and a blue HUNG on her heart.

དཀར་པོ་ༀ་གྱིས་བྱིན་གྱིས་རློབས༔

KAR PO   OM   GYI   JIN GYI LOB
white#   OM   of   receiving blessing
I receive blessings of the white letter OM.

དམར་པོ་ཨཱཿ ཡིས་བྱིན་གྱིས་རློབས༔

MAR PO   AA   YI   JIN GYI LOB
red#   AA   of   receiving blessing
I receive blessings of the red letter AA.

སྔོན་པོ་ཧཱུྃ་གིས་བྱིན་གྱིས་རློབས༔

NGON PO HUNG   GI   JIN GYI LOB

blue#   HUNG   of   receiving blessing

I receive blessings of the blue letter HUNG.

#)   white, red and blue rays of light come from the letters OM,
      AA and HUNG. They melt in my own forehead, throat and
      heart and purify all sins and obscurations of my body, speech
      and mind.

སྐུ་གསུང་ཐུགས་ཀྱིས་བྱིན་ཆེན་ཕོབ༔

KU   SUNG   THUG KYI   JIN CHEN PHOB

body   speech   mind   of   receiving great blessing

I receive the great blessings of her body, speech and mind.

མ་ཡུམ་ཆེན་གོ་འཕང་ཐོབ་པར་ཤོག༔

MA YUM   CHEN GO PANGTHOB PAR   SHOG

mother   great   stage   gain   must be

I must gain the same stage as the great mother.

OM. I pray to Machig Labdron, the mother.
AA. I pray to Machig Labdron, the mother.
HUNG. I pray to Machig Labdron, the mother.
I receive blessing of the white letter OM.
I receive blessing of the red letter AA.
I receive blessing of the blue letter HUNG.
I receive the great blessings of her body, speech and mind.
I must gain the same stage as the great mother.

Don Sal Melong

Garab Dorje

Dedication of Merit

༄༅། །དགེ་བ་འདི་ཡིས་མྱུར་དུ་བདག །
།པདྨ་འབྱུང་གནས་འགྲུབ་གྱུར་ནས། །
།འགྲོ་བ་གཅིག་ཀྱང་མ་ལུས་པ། །
།དེ་ཡི་ས་ལ་འགོད་པར་ཤོག །

By this merit may I quickly
Become inseparable from Padmasambhava
And lead all sentient beings without exception
To that state.

Prayer to Spread the Dharma

ཉེར་འཚེ་མ་ལུས་ཞི་བ་དང་།

མཐུན་རྐྱེན་ནམ་མཁའི་མཛོད་བཞིན་དུ།

རྒྱལ་དབང་པདྨ་འབྱུང་གནས་ཀྱི།

བསྟན་པ་ཡུན་རིང་འབར་གྱུར་ཅིག།

ༀ་ཨཱཿ ཧཱུྃ་བཛྲ་གུ་རུ་པདྨ་སིདྡྷི་ཧཱུྃཿ

All difficulties without exception being pacified, and
with harmonious situations like the treasure of the sky,
Padmasambhava's, the lord of the Jinas'
doctrines must live long and shine brightly!
Indestructible Guru Padmasambhava having the three Kayas,
grant real attainments!

Prayer for the Swift Rebirth of His Holiness Khordong Terchen Tulku Chhimed Rigdzin Rinpoche

ཙཱཀྱོ

Don Sal Melong

༄༅། །ཨོཾ་སྭ་སྟི།

ཧྲ་མེད་མཚོ་སྐྱེས་རྒྱལ་བའི་རིང་ལུགས་མཆོག །

བཀའ་གཏེར་ཟབ་རྒྱས་སྒྲུབ་མཐའ་དག་བསམ་མི་ཁྱབ།

སྒྱུར་མཛད་འཆི་བ་མེད་པའི་རིག་འཛིན་རྗེ།

ཡང་སྤྲུལ་མྱུར་འབྱོན་མཛད་ཕྲིན་ལྷུན་གྲུབ་ཤོག །

Wonderful! Chhimed Rigdzin, you spread the inconceivable instructions of initiation and teachings of the Buddha's oral lineage and the hidden treasures, belonging to the ancient tradition of the unsurpassed lake-born Buddha. May your Tulku incarnation come quickly and may all activities be spontaneously accomplished!

Written by H.H. Dilgo Khyentse Rinpoche as a long-life prayer, and altered by Chhimed Rigdzin Rinpoche shortly before his death.

FURTHER READING

There are now many important texts on Dzogchen available in English. Here are few suggestions covering a wide range of styles and periods.

THE GOLDEN LETTERS: The Tibetan Teachings of Garab Dorje, First Dzogchen Master, trans. & ed. by *John Reynolds*; foreword by *Namkhai Norbu*, 389 pp. Snow Lion Publications, 1996, ISBN: 1559390506

THE PRACTICE OF DZOGCHEN by *Longchen Rabjam*, intro. & trans. by *Tulku Thondup*, 488 pp., Snow Lion Publications, 2002, ISBN: 1559391790

THE PHILOSOPHICAL VIEW OF THE GREAT PERFECTION IN THE TIBETAN BON RELIGION by *Donatella Rossi*, 315 pp., Snow Lion Publications, 1999, ISBN: 1559391294

NATURAL GREAT PERFECTION. Dzogchen Teachings and Vajra Songs by *Nyoshul Khenpo Rinpoche*, trans. & ed. by *Lama Surya Das*, 150 pp., Snow Lion Publications, 1995, ISBN: 1559390492

PRIMORDIAL EXPERIENCE: An Introduction to rDzogs-chen Meditation by *Manjushrimitra*, trans. by *Namkhai Norbu & Kennard Lipman*, 192 pp., Shambhala Publications, 1987, ISBN: 157062898X

RIGBAI KUJYUG – The Six Vajra Verses, An Oral Commentary by *Namkhai Norbu Rinpoche*, Edited by *Cheh-Ngee Goh*, 136 pp., Rinchen Editions Pte Ltd, Singapore, 1990, ISBN: 981-00-1610-7

THE SUPREME SOURCE: The Fundamental Tantra of Dzogchen Semde by *Chogyal Namkhai Norbu & Adriano Clemente*, 325 pp., Snow Lion Publications, 1999, ISBN: 1559391200

THE PRECIOUS TREASURY OF THE WAY OF ABIDING by *Longchen Rabjam* (Longchenpa), 318 pp., Padma Publishing, 1998, ISBN: 1881847098

SIMPLE BEING: Texts in the Dzogchen Tradition by *Chetsangpa, Patrul Rinpoche, Chhimed Rigdzin Lama, Rigdzin Godem, Nuden Dorje, Padmasambhava*, intro. & trans. by *James Low*, 175 pp.,Vajra Press, 1998, ISBN: 0 9532845 0 6